Mr. Van Dooren lectured on prayer when I was a student at Bodenseehof in 1979-1980. He won my immediate respect as a man of prayer who practiced what he preached. He left a great impression on me. When I later joined the staff of Bodenseehof, Mr. Van Dooren took me under his wing whenever he came to visit. I'll never forget the Sunday evening when he stood up to share with the students. Before he prayed for us all, standing in front of this group of squirrelly young students he said, "I'm sorry that I have only made it this far in my growth and walk with the Lord." Then he prayed. I was stunned by the man's humility and faithfulness to the Lord and the way in which he opened the scriptures with such reverence, and always pointing us to Christ through whatever passage he addressed. One summer when I was leading a conference Mr. Van Dooren called the office from England just to let me know that he was praying for me that week. He was a continual source of encouragement until he went home to be with the One who loved him so deeply and whom he loved in return. I'm delighted that the seeds which were sown in Mr. Van Dooren's lectures decades ago are still bearing fruit to this day in the lives of those who sat under his teaching. It may well be said of Mr. Van Dooren, "Though he is dead, he still speaks." (Heb. 11:4)

Peter Reid, Director
Christian Youth Center and Bible School, Bodenseehof, Germany
Torchbearers International General Director

THE BEST OF CAPERNWRAY

NOTES ON THE OLD TESTAMENT
and More

VOLUME 1

L.A.T. VAN DOOREN

Transcribed by Miriam Maranzenboim

Copyright © 2020 Miriam Maranzenboim

ALL RIGHTS RESERVED. This book contains material protected under International and Federal Copyright Laws and Treaties. Any unauthorized reprint or use of this material is prohibited. No part of this book may be reproduced or transmitted in any form or by any means, electronic or mechanical, including photocopying, recording, or by any information storage and retrieval system without express written permission from the author/publisher.

Paperback ISBN: 978-1-64184-334-8
eBook ISBN: 978-1-64184-335-5

"Dedicated especially to the thousands
of people over the past
70+ years
Who have been touched by the ministry of
CAPERNWRAY"

ABOUT CAPERNWRAY

Major and Mrs. Thomas bought Capernwray Hall, a former stately home for a family of five (and thirty servants!), on 11th September 1946 with a desire to see it full of youth *"coming to a saving knowledge of the Lord Jesus Christ"* and as a place where *"Christians may find a warm and happy Christian fellowship."* Since then around 150,000 guests or students from 50 countries have stayed here. Now there are branches of the Bible school and/or conference centers in more than 20 different countries.

ABOUT THE AUTHOR

Mr. L.A.T. Van Dooren was associated with Capernwray Hall since its inception. He was one of the Directors of the Capernwray Hall Conference Center and had been the principal of the Capernwray Bible School since its founding in 1949, until 1975 when he became president of the Capernwray Bible Schools throughout the world.

He had the opportunity of ministry not only in England but through all Western and South Eastern European countries, the Middle East, Israel, North Africa, Australia, New Zealand, the Philippines, the Far East and India.

Mr. Van Dooren's writing ministry was particularly extensive in the field of evangelism and in the preparation of material for young Christians. The Latimer tracts and booklets which he wrote were translated into many languages.

In addition to leading the studies of the Capernwray Bible School, he also promoted the Operational Bible Study Correspondence Courses and is the author of 16 books. His book, *Introducing the Old Testament* is unavailable and was endorsed by Professor F.F. Bruce and Dr. A. Skevington Wood.

It's obvious from these intensive notes on the Bible that he devoted most of his life to studying it and teaching it. This book also contains his notes on General Background to the Bible and Structure of the Old Testament and the Intertestamental period.

TABLE OF CONTENTS

Introduction to the Study of the Bible. 1
Period between the Old Testament and New Testament 19
Genesis 32
Exodus 48
Leviticus 56
Numbers. 68
Deuteronomy 75
Joshua. 80
Judges 90
Ruth 97
I Samuel 101
II Samuel. 106
1 Kings 111
2 Kings 115
1 Chronicles 120
2 Chronicles 125
Historical Background – Preparatory to the Study
of the Books of Ezra, Nehemiah and Esther 130
Ezra. 132
Nehemiah 136
Esther 140

Job	143
Psalms	149
Proverbs	154
Ecclesiastes	157
Song Of Solomon	162
Isaiah	166
Jeremiah	172
Lamentations	178
Ezekiel	181
Daniel	187
Hosea	192
Joel	196
Amos	201
Obadiah	206
Jonah	210
Micah	215
Nahum	220
Habakkuk	224
Zephaniah	228
Haggai	231
Zechariah	235
Malachi	242
Acknowledgments	247
About the Transcriber Miriam Maranzenboim	249

INTRODUCTION TO THE STUDY OF THE BIBLE

GENERAL BACKGROUND TO THE BIBLE AND STRUCTURE OF THE OLD TESTAMENT

The Derivation and Meaning of the name "The Bible"

English form of plural Latin word 'Biblia' – taken from plural Greek word meaning Books, comes from the name of a plant 'Byblos', which derived its name from a town in Phoenicia which the Greeks knew as Byblos. A Biblion was a roll of papyrus or Byblos. This reed plant was used as material for early writings. Wide strips of the plant were laid out and other strips were laid across and thus the two rows joined together, making a piece of writing material. These pieces were joined together and rolled up in the form of a scroll and called in Greek a 'Biblos' or 'Biblion.' In the New Testament, the word 'Biblion' simply means a 'roll' or 'book'; plural is 'Biblia'. The Old and New Testament soon became known to the Greek speaking Christians as 'ta biblia', that is, 'The Books'. Later, Latin speaking Christians borrowed the term – treated it as a singular and from the Latin name the English word 'Bible' is derived.

The original plural significance of the name must not be overlooked. Jerome describes the Bible as "the Divine Library". It is many books written by many different authors over many centuries, but there is one spiritual purpose and unity of thought. It is a Library – yet one Book.

Parchment (or Vellum) comes from the skin of an animal such as sheep, goat, etc., - more durable – name comes from Pergamum where there was at one time an industry in this material.

A book with pages was not in use in New Testament times – appeared shortly after, and this was known as a "Codex".

PERIOD OF WRITING

One thousand five hundred years; the oldest Books being the Books of Moses and Job. The last written Book was probably the Gospel according to John, written about 90 or 100 A.D.

NUMBER OF BOOKS

Sixty-six. Old Testament – thirty nine. New Testament – twenty seven. It is a good practice to memorize the correct order of these.

WRITERS

Old Testament – about thirty. New Testament – probably nine, thus making nearly forty human writers from totally different stations in life. Name as many as possible of these writers, their original occupations, the country and place there they wrote.

ORIGINAL LANGUAGES

Hebrew, Aramaic and Greek

HEBREW

Not a dead language; official language of Israel. Ancient and modern Hebrew are more alike than English of Chaucer's day and modern English. It is one of the earliest alphabetic languages, (there are those who consider it to be the earliest) which in the providence of God was available for recording His written revelation to man. A language peculiarly suitable for transmission of the Divine revelation by its use of vivid idioms and forthright utterances. Indirect speech is unknown in Biblical Hebrew – all speeches reported in direct form whether the words were the actual words spoken or represent the general purport of what was said.

Hebrew uses daring anthropomorphisms when speaking of God – Exodus 33:23, etc. Nations, groups of people are frequently given a name and personality. For example, you find reference to Jacob, Esau, Judah, Ephraim, Manasseh, etc., when not these individuals are referred to but their descendants. A form of extreme emphasis is a feature of the Hebrew language. For instance, Malachi 1:2-3 which Hebraism is preserved in Luke 14:26.

An important feature of Hebrew is that "although the Old Testament extends over a period of a thousand years, there is almost no difference between the language of the oldest parts and that of the latest." T.H. Weir

International Standard Biblical Encyclopaedia. When dealing with destructive criticism, it is important to remember that it is not possible to date with certainty any of the writings by the character of the language alone.

About 200 B.C. the Square characters were introduced, to be later followed (about 500 A.D.) by vowel points. The scheme finally established and now in the use was the work of the Masoretes of Tiberias, Masoretes meaning 'Masters of the tradition' and represents the pronunciation of Hebrew vowels current from the end of the eighth century onwards. Absence of vowel signs in ancient Hebrew sometimes accounts for minor variations of texts; for example, Genesis 47:31 and Hebrews 11:21. The Hebrew word for 'bed' and 'staff' have the same consonants. The quotations in Hebrews come from the Greek version of Old Testament. The Scribes translating into the Greek read in the vowels a a e, giving the word 'staff'. The Hebrew Scribes, from which our Old Testament text was received, read in a i a, giving the word 'bed'.

ARAMAIC

Called 'Syrian language', 2 Kings 18:26. 'Syriack,' Daniel 2:4 sometimes miscalled Chaldaic from mistaken inference in Daniel 2:4. Aramaic portions Ezra 4:8 to 6:1; 7:12-26; Jeremiah 10:11; Daniel 2:4 to 7:28. The first reference in the Bible to Aramaic in Genesis 31:47. Laban used Aramaic name and Jacob the Hebrew name, both meaning 'Cairn of Witness'. The Cairn may have been near the linguistic frontier. In view of close connection between ancestors of the Israelites and Aramaic speaking people, it is not surprising to find many Aramaisms in Old Testament Hebrew at an early date. For example, Judges 5:11 – 'rehearse' (c1100 A.D.) The name Aramaic comes from Aram, the Hebrew word for Syria. Important stage in history of Aramaic language in the eighth century B.C. at that time adopted as the language of diplomatic intercourse in Assyrian Empire. Examples of this 2 Kings 18:17-37; Isaiah 36:3-22. In these passages (700 B.C.) Reb-shakeh (literally 'cup bearer' – it is a title, not a personal name) addressed Hezekiah's delegation so loudly in Hebrew that they feared lest the citizens on the wall listening would hear and be demoralized, thus, virtually, they said 'use usual diplomatic language, for we understand it' – 2 Kings 18:26. Aramaic continued as Diplomatic language until the overthrow of the Persian Empire by Alexander the Great in 331 B.C. In the light of this it is interesting to note Aramaic portions of Ezra comprises official state correspondence.

During Babylonian captivity, the Jewish exiles picked up this language; it was language of common intercourse with other people with whom they mixed. Upon the return of the captives to Palestine, they took the language back and probably found it had also been largely adopted even by those who had remained in the land. Many born in exile may not have learned the Hebrew language of their forefathers. Hebrew remained the ecclesiastical language. Haggai, Zechariah, Malachi all prophesied and wrote tin Hebrew, but language position had become reverse to that in Hezekiah's day. In the Post-exile days few of the common people know Hebrew but all understood Aramaic, hence Nehemiah 8:8 (note also 8:2 and 3). It is thought that 'Distinctly' is 'with an interpretation', so that the people understood the reading.

Aramaic remained the vernacular of Palestine until Arab conquest in the seventh century. It was, therefore, the customary language of our Lord, His apostles and of the early Church in Palestine. Many Aramaic words have been taken over and translated into the New Testament; e.g. Mark 5:41; 7:34; 15:34, the latter being quotation from Aramaic.

'Abba' Father is an Aramaic word which found its way into Hebrew as well. It is the affectionate term for intimate use within the family – Mark 14:36; Romans 8:15; Galatians 4:6.

"Marana the' – I Corinthians 16:22, meaning 'The Lord comes' or 'Our Lord, come.'

'Mammon' comes from Aramaic 'Mamona' meaning that in which one puts his trust. Other instances of words from the Aramaic are 'Golgotha' - (the skull), 'Gabbatha' – (hill), Martha – (mistress), Thomas – (twin). In the Gospels and Acts Aramaic idioms are to be found (as would be expected) as these writings contain the sayings of our Lord and others who spoke Aramaic. This does not, however, imply that they were originally written in Aramaic.

GREEK

If, as shown above, Aramaic appears to have been the common tongue of our Lord and New Testament writers, the question arises, 'Why is it not the language of the New Testament?'

Old Testament revelation committed particularly to one nation as a trust – (Romans 3:2) therefore recorded in that nation's language. New Testament revelation not intended to be restricted but committed to all nations – Luke 2:3-32; 24:47. Most appropriate language, therefore, would be the one most widely known. In God's providence, a suitable language lay ready to hand. Greek culture is well known. The Greeks were united under Philip of Macedonia in 338 B.C. His son, Alexander the Great, extended the Empire and thus carried the language throughout the then known world. The differences between the various Greek dialects were in this process slowly eliminated. In the last three centuries B.C. Hellenistic Greek, the 'common speech' or 'koine dialektos' became the most widely known language. It was the official language of the Empires into which the Grecian Empire was divided after Alexander the Great's death in 323 B.C. The Roman Empire which followed was bi-lingual, Latin, being the language of the Army in all parts and Greek, the common language of the streets, sports arena, trade and foreign intercourse. Palestine became incorporated in the Roman Empire in 63 B.C. as part of the province of Syria. To the educated, classical Greek was the language of culture and ancient classics. To the lower classes and slaves, the common tongue, or colloquial Greek was the language of their birth. The difference might be compared to that between Elizabethan and present day English with its modern tendencies.

It was at one time thought that the New Testament Greek was a special and peculiar language. Indeed, it was once called 'the language of the Holy Ghost'. Modern research and discovery has, however, proved it to be the language of the common people, the everyday speech of the Roman world of its day, the language in which everyday correspondence and personal letters were written. It was a language rich in style, elegance, idioms and exact expression which give it a place of eminence amongst languages and rendered it admirable for the communicating of God's revelation to men.

In the New Testament the influence of the Greek of the Septuagint is manifest. Also Aramaic influence derived from the Palestinian vernacular.

BIBLICAL MANUSCRIPTS

Manuscript, as the name implies, means written by hand. All original MSS now lost, but there are thousands of old Hebrew and Greek MSS scattered mainly throughout libraries of Europe.

OLD TESTAMENT MSS

In 1948 several ancient MSS were discovered in jars in a cave at Ain Feshkha, near Jericho. Most important, a complete parchment scroll of the Book of Isaiah in Hebrew. Professor W.F. Albright of John Hopkin's University USA dates the MS the <u>Second century B.C.</u> "The script of this parchment is easily thousands years older than that of the oldest Hebrew Biblical roll hitherto known". Among parchments more recently found in the Cave are portions of Genesis, Leviticus, Deuteronomy, Judges; also fragments of the Book of Daniel and Commentary on Habakkuk.

The previous earliest MS of Hebrew Old Testament is a Codex of the Prophets of Leningrad. It is dated 916 A.D. Another early Codex of the whole of the Old Testament belongs to early eleventh century, also at Leningrad. Oxford has another Codex almost as old. The British Museum has Codex of the Hebrew Pentateuch usually dated ninth century. There is a Cairo Codex of the Prophets completed in 895 A.D. The question might well be asked 'Why the few really ancient Hebrew MSS?'

This is accounted for by the reverent care with which old Jewish Rabbis treated the text. When it was too old or worn for further use, it was given an honorable burial, but before this, they were stored for longer or shorter periods in a 'Genizah' – a room attached to a Synagogue where documents no longer in use were stored. Genizah means a hiding place. One such Genizah attached to a Synagogue in old Cairo was discovered to still contain its ancient MSS until these were made available to scholars in the latter half of the last century.

It has been stated that it was at the end of the eighth century A.D. that the vowel points were finally established, thus settling the pronunciation and various readings. This is known as the Masoretic text. Meticulous care was taken to avoid any scribal errors. It was such that the scribes would count the number of times each letter of the alphabet appeared in each Book; they would mark out the middle letter of the Pentateuch and of the whole Hebrew Bible. "Everything countable seems to have been counted" – Mr. Wheeler Robinson "Ancient and English Versions of the Bible 1940" p. 29. When the Masoretic text was finally established by these means it appeared that all previous copies of scriptures were withdrawn from use and confined to the Genizah. It will, therefore, be seen that although the MSS of the Hebrew Old Testament are of a comparatively late date, the text is thoroughly trustworthy.

NEW TESTAMENT MSS

New Testament MSS number about 4,000. By comparison, it is possible to be almost sure of the exact content of the originals. No other ancient literature is so well attested as is the New Testament, both by the number of MSS and also by the age of existing MSS. It is interesting to compare with such writings Caesar's 1st Gallic Wars and the Histories of Tecitus, etc. For instance, the History of Herodotus – (480 – 425 B.C.) is known to us through MSS of the ninth century. Nobody, however, doubts the History of Herodotus, although the earliest MSS are thirteen hundred years later than their originals. In the John Rylands Library, Manchester, there is a papyrus Codex containing verses of John 18 which dates from the first half of the second century. In the Chester Beatty Biblical papyri there are MSS which belong to the first and second half of the third century.

THREE MOST FAMOUS NEW TESTAMENT MSS ARE:

CODEX SINITICUS (Codex Aleph)

This is a parchment copy of the whole Greek Bible, although a good part of the Old Testament has been lost – dated from the fourth century.

CODEX ALEXANDRINUS (Codex A)

Written in the fifth century is another copy of the Greek Bible. Both the above are in the British Museum.

CODEX VATICANUS (Codex B)

Dates from the fourth century and is chief treasure of Vatican library.

There are various other MSS containing parts of the New Testament dating from the fourth and fifth century.

THE OLD AND NEW TESTAMENTS OR COVENANTS

The translators would probably have passed on a more correct term if they had used the term "Agreement" or "Covenant". These are scriptural terms – Exodus 24:8. Moses acted as mediator and solemnized the Covenant between God and Israel whereby Israel because God's people and Jehovah became their God. The Covenant was by reason of the

Lord's promise of grace made to Abraham. Receiving the Law did not make them God's people. They received the Law because they were His people and God gave them the Law as their rule of life.

The Lord Jesus Christ inaugurates the new Covenant between God and Himself which was ratified by His own blood and issues in blessing to all mankind. Mark 14:24; 1 Cor. 11:25; 2 Cor. 3:6.

The Old Testament is often spoken of as of law – 'this do and thou shalt live' – and the New Testament as of grace – 'believe on the Lord Jesus Christ and thou shalt be saved'. It is necessary to remember that there is much of grace in the Old Testament and that in the New Testament, when a man is saved, God reveals primarily through the Epistles how a man should live as a new creation in Christ.

CANON

Greek word meaning 'measuring rod' or 'rule'. Came to mean a standard rule by which things were judged. It is often said by unbelievers that certain Councils met and decided which Books should be included in the Bible and which should not. This is not in accord with facts. The Canon of Scripture grew and the Boks which were stamped with Divine Authority became generally accepted in process of time. Formal ratification of the Old Testament Books was made at Jamnia in A.D. 90 and 118 by Jewish Councils, although they had been accepted as we now have them prior to our Lord's Day. Likewise, when the Church Council of Carthage met in A.D. 397 and listed the 27 Books of the New Testament, it did not confer upon them any authority which they did not already have. It simply recorded their established authority as a necessary answer to false or heretical teachers. Dr. Foakes Jackson "The Church assuredly did not make the New Testament, the two grew up together" – "History of Church History" 1939 p. 21.

The Muratorian Fragment (discovered in 1740 by L.A. Muratori) which is dated between A.D. 160 and 170 lists all the books of the New Testament with the exception of Hebrews, 1 and 2 Peter and 3 John. Athanasius in his Festal Letter of A.D. 367 listed the 27 Books of the New Testament. Jerome and Augustine likewise shortly afterwards.

Previously, Irenaeus, A.D. 135-200, a disciple of Polycarp, who was a disciple of the Apostle John, had attested the authenticity of all the New Testament except Philemon and James, 2nd Peter, 2 and 3 John, Jude and Hebrews. Similarly, both Origen A.D. 230, and Eusebius A.D. 270 – 340, mention certain of these Epistles were disputed by some. It is important to remember that there would not be the speed of transcribing and circulation as today. Certain Churches would have certain Books, not knowing the other writings until such time as another teacher brought them. In such cases the writings would first be received with caution, as there were many spurious writings in circulation to which the name of an Apostle had been appended.

<u>It is essential to remember that the Authority of the Word of God is derived from its Authenticity.</u> Authenticity precedes Canonicity. When the Books were Canonized they did not assume Authenticity, nor as a result of that did they become Authoritative. <u>It was because they were Authentic</u> and <u>Authoritative that they were Canonized.</u> AUTHENTICITY PRECEDES CANONICITY.

The early Christians (as are all true believers) being indwelt by the Holy Spirit, were guided by the Spirit in that which they received and that which they rejected. It is well to remember that the witness of the Holy Spirit to the Divine Authority of the Scripture is both to the individual and to the Church as a community. John chapter 8:42-48; 10:27; 16:13; 1 John 4:1-6; 1 Cor. 2:14-15; 1 Cor. 14:37-38.

ANCIENT VERSIONS

A MSS is a copy of the scriptures in the original language. A Version is a translation from the original tongue into another language or a copy of a translation.

A. <u>The Septuagint.</u> Originally this translation was of the Pentateuch only – reputed to be by 72 translators of Alexandria in the third century B.C. By the time of Origen, early third century A.D., the name applied to the whole Greek translation of Old Testament.

B. <u>The Syriac.</u> Old Testament was probably translated about 200 A.D. The New Testament rather earlier. No direct information as by whom the translation was made. This version used by those who went eastward as far as India, etc., and the Nestorian mission to China. Written in a distinctive form of Aramaic, generally known as Christian Aramaic.

C. <u>The Vulgate.</u> Latin Bible translated by Jerome in 386-405. There had been many previous translations of the New Testament into Latin and Jerome's work was a revision of these, and a new translation <u>direct from the Hebrew</u> in the case of the Old Testament. The Vulgate has been the standard Latin Bible of the West ever since. From this version the early English versions were translated, e.g., - Wycliffe's.

D. <u>The Samaritan Pentateuch.</u> The Samaritans regard the Pentateuch as canonical. Not many substantial differences between the Samaritan Pentateuch and the Orthodox Hebrew, although many minor differences. It was written in ancient Hebrew script and has value in confirming the Masoretic text of the Pentateuch. The Samaritan text goes back many centuries prior to the Masoretic.

MODERN VERSIONS

It is not proposed to deal with the way in which the English Bible was made available; suffice it to say that the Authorized Version remains the translation which is generally used in England. The Revised Version is more accurate in places but lacks something of the grandeur of the A.V.

The Standard Revised Version has recently made its appearance and has had a mixed reception. There are a variety of versions in modern English. Dr. Weymouth's translation of the New Testament will be found of considerable help.

L.A.T. VAN DOOREN

CRITICISM OF THE BIBLE

Takes two forms: Lower or Textual Criticism and Higher Criticism.

<u>Lower or Textual Criticism</u> based on comparison of MSS in original Hebrew and Greek and the early versions in other languages. This accounts for attention occasionally being drawn to different readings, many minor differences but the more MSS available, while increasing the number of minor differences, also confirms the accuracy of the text as a whole. Dr. Hort states "In all these voluminous writings which have been copied times without number, we may be sure that in regard to the New Testament the variation of any importance amount to less than 1000th part of the entire text, while the Hebrew MSS show still less variation. Not one doctrine is affected in the slightest way." – *Introduction to the New Testament*, p. 2. Sir Frederick Kenyon in his books *The Story of the Bible* and *The Bible and Archaeology* states "It is reassuring at the end to find that the general result of all these discoveries and the study is to strengthen the proof of the authenticity of the scriptures, and our conviction that we have in our hands in substantial integrity, the veritable Word of God." "Both the Authenticity and the general integrity of the Books of the New Testament may be regarded as finally established." This criticism has vindicated the authority of the text that we now have.

<u>Higher Criticism.</u> So called because it deals with the writing higher up in the stream of its existence. For example, it asks such questions as "Who wrote?", "When written?" "To whom?" "Where was it written?" "Why was it written?"

It investigates questions of authorship, date, etc. By reason of the destructive conclusions often reached on ill-founded grounds by unspiritual men, the term "higher critic" has become one of ill report and almost synonymous with unbelief and rejection of the scriptures as the Word of God. Much of this so-called criticism sets out not so much to criticize as to establish a theory. What is sometimes termed 'cautious scholarship' is frequently more correctly 'skeptical scholarship'.

It has often been pointed out that both Testaments reveal a similar structure each having a three-fold division as follows:

Historic	Doctrinal or Ethical	Prophetic
O.T. to Esther	Job to Song of Solomon	Isaiah to Malachi
N.T. Matthew to Acts	Romans to Jude	Revelation

This division must not, however, be considered arbitrary. There is considerable overlapping of subject matter.

THE OLD TESTAMENT

Thirty nine Books.

The Hebrew Bible with which our Lord was familiar comprised 24 Books. Each of the following were considered as one Book:

1 and 2 Samuel. 1 and 2 Kings. 1 and 2 Chronicles. Ezra and Nehemiah.

The Twelve Minor Prophets.

Josephus and Jerome both wrote of it as 22 Books by joining Lamentations to Jeremiah and Ruth to Judges.

The Three Major Divisions of Hebrew Bible are:

1. The LAW – Torah – Five Books: Genesis to Deuteronomy

2. The PROPHETS – Nebhuim. This section sub-divided:

    The Former Prophets: Joshua, Judges, Samuel, Kings

    The Latter Prophets: Isaiah, Jeremiah, Ezekiel, Book of the Twelve

3. The WRITINGS – Kethubim – Greek name Hagiographa meaning 'Sacred or Holy writings': Psalms, Proverbs, Job

The Five Rolls: Song of Solomon, Ruth, Lamentations, Ecclesiastes, Esther, Daniel, Ezra-Nehemiah, Chronicles.

This section was often known as the Psalms either by reason of Psalms being the first book in the division or because it was the longest. The Lord Jesus Christ referred to this three-fold division of the Hebrew Bible in Luke 24:44. It has been suggested that arrangement of the Hebrew Bible was according to the order in which it was built up, collected and accepted as canonical. The Five Rolls were read at the respective Jewish Festivals as follows:

The Song of Solomon at Passover : Ruth at Feast of Weeks or Pentecost:

Ecclesiastes at the Feast of Tabernacles : Esther at the Feast of Purim.

Lamentations was recited on Anniversary of destruction of Jerusalem.

THE GROUPING OF THE OLD TESTAMENT IN THE ENGLISH BIBLE

Based on Latin Vulgate, which in turn is based on the Septuagint and is according to subject matter:

1. The Law, that is the Pentateuch.

   Five Books : Genesis to Deuteronomy. Written Pre-Canaan period.

2. History – Twelve Books.

   Joshua to Esther. Nine written Canaan. Three written in Post-exile period (i.e., after expulsion and repatriation in Canaan)

3. Poetry – Five Books: Job to Song of Solomon

4. Prophecy – Seventeen Books (5 and 12); Isaiah to Malachi.

A. Major. Five Books divided in the center by Lamentations both historically (Isaiah and Jeremiah being pre-exile and Ezekiel and Daniel during exile) and positional. Isaiah, Jeremiah, Ezekiel and Daniel between them determine the main outline of prophecy. Isaiah writes of the suffering and Exaltation of the Savior. Jeremiah, pronouncing the overthrow of Israel also tells of the coming 'Branch and Restorer.' The Lamentations follow and then Ezekiel speaks of the Judgment, the departed Glory and finally the Coming Glory.

Daniel gives an orderly program of the Messiah coming, being cut off and Coming Again.

This briefly, is the main theme of Old Testament prophecy.

B. <u>Minor</u>. Twelve Books not minor because of less value. The term has to do with the length and not importance of the Books.

The Old Testament is often disparaged. August says 'The New is in the Old contained, the Old is in the New explained". "In the Books of the Law the quest is for the Priest who will abide; in the Historic Books for a King who will excel: in the Prophetic Books for a Prophet of perfect vision. Open the New Testament and now here is One who is Prophet, Priest and King. The Old Testament asks eagerly where is the Lamb for the burnt offering; the New Testament answers joyfully, 'Behold the Lamb of God who taketh away the sin of the world'. Over the Old Testament write 'anticipation', over the New 'realization'." R.D. Johnston.

Both Old and New Testaments are indispensable. The one cannot be fully understood apart from the other. The Old Testament was our Lord's Bible. He constantly referred to these scriptures and quoted them, thus revealing an intimate knowledge of their contents. If the Old Testament scriptures were indispensable to our Lord, how much more needful are they to us. Refer to Luke 16:27-31.

Students should write down as many as possible of our Lord's allusions to the Old Testament. When reading the New Testament, be ready to note the outstanding quotations and references. It may be helpful to use in the New Testament a special marking against all Old Testament quotations and direct references.

Rejection of the Old Testament invariably paves the way for doubting and rejection of the New. The more we love Christ, the more we find Him in the Old Testament. It is the unfolding of God's redemptive purposes for mankind; it is God's illustration book. It has been said the pictures of Christ are found in the Old Testament, the Person of Christ in the Gospels and the Preaching of Christ in the Epistles. The very first verse of the New Testament assumes knowledge of and an acquaintance with the Old – Matthew 1:1.

<u>The Morality of Old Testament</u>: Needful to remember that like all revelation it is progressive according to man's power to comprehend. It is even so in the New Testament, our Lord said "I have many things to say unto you but ye cannot bear them now". John 16:12.

An important contribution of the Old Testament which is often overlooked is that it <u>reveals God's governmental dealings with nations</u>.

Old Testament history ceases at approximately 400 B.C. thus leaving an unrecorded period of about 400 years. Students should acquaint themselves with the events and developments of this period.

OLD TESTAMENT GEOGRAPHY AND HISTORY OF OTHER NATIONS

It is a considerable help to the understanding of the Old Testament to know the location of important Cities, places, etc., in the Promised Land and other countries. This should be studied from a good map: a useful and instructive exercise being to list names of the most familiar cities and places and locate their position. It is equally important to know the position of those nations which surrounded Israel and whose history touches the story of the Chosen People. Therefore, observe the position of the world powers such as Egypt, The Hittites, Phoenicia, Syria, Assyria, Babylonia and Medo-Persian.

The location and derivation of lesser nations with which Israel came into contact should be also noted (by reference to a map and concordance) e.g., the Amalekites, Ammonites, Amorites, Canaanites, Edomites, Midianites, Moabites, Philistines.

CHAPTER AND VERSE DIVISIONS

It is necessary to remember these are artificial, an aid to reference but never in the mind of the writer. The Hebrew Bible had an arrangement of verses earlier than that fixed by the Masoretic period which is the one that has come down to us. 23,100 verses in the Old Testament.

THE BEST OF CAPERNWRAY

The Bible was divided into chapters in 1244 to 1250 by Cardinal Hugo de Sancto Caro; the New Testament into verses in 1551 by Sir Robert Stephanus. The Geneva Bible (sometimes called the Breeches Bible because of the translation Genesis 3:7 "made themselves breeches") in 1560 was the first Bible to have verses throughout and italics. The latter; signifying words not in the original. Authorized Bible 1611 had marginal references; these had appeared in a small scale in a Bible of 1599. Chapter headings were written by Miles Smith, one of the translators of the Authorized Version. The Revised Version of 1885 adopted paragraphs and this has been followed by the majority of the modern versions.

THE TITLES OF THE BOOKS

The titles found at the commencement of each book have been added at a date later than the actual writing.

REVISION EXERCISE.

1. Explain why the Bible has been called 'the Divine Library'.

2. How does one account for the comparatively few Old Testament MSS which date earlier than the ninth century?

3. Although they are of later date, why are the Old Testament MSS trustworthy?

4. Approximately how many ancient MSS are there of the New Testament?

5. Give the three-fold division of the Hebrew Bible and a New Testament reference to it.

6. Write out as many names as possible of writers of Old Testament Books and their original occupation.

7. How would you deal with the objection "Why should I accept the Bible? It is only a collection of books which certain men have decided should be preserved"?

8. Give the four-fold division of the Old Testament as in the English Bible and name the Books in each.

9. State an occasion when our Lord gave three direct quotations from the Old Testament.

10. Name at least six Old Testament characters to whom our Lord made direct reference.

11. How far should we be guided in our reading by the chapter or verse divisions of the scriptures?

PERIOD BETWEEN THE OLD TESTAMENT AND NEW TESTAMENT

I. HISTORIC DEVELOPMENTS

From the close of Old Testament History (The Book of Nehemiah) to the opening of the New Testament there is a period of approximately 400 years. During this time many changes took place which had differing effects on Palestine and the Jewish nation, so that when the New Testament commences, there is a tremendous difference to the closing conditions of the Old Testament. The reader of the New Testament finds he is in a new world. It is helpful to know a little of the causes of these changes.

Historically, the four hundred years may be summarized into Five Periods

I. PERSIAN DOMINATION. 538-330 B.C.

Persian domination of the world commenced in 538 B.C. with the fall of Babylon, and therefore for the purpose of these notes, extends from the days of Nehemiah to Alexander's Conquest in 330 B.C. It was a time of comparative peace. Resulting from Nehemiah's firm stand that the inhabitants of Samaria should have no share in the rebuilding of Jerusalem, a temple was built in Mount Gerizim and a form of Samaritan worship established.

II. GRECIAN OR MACEDONIAN PERIOD. 330-167 B.C.

Alexander the Great became King at 20 years old and reigned from 335 to 323 B.C. when he died of Malaria. His rise and conquest of the known world is foretold in Daniel 8:1-8 and 10:20.

It is stated that when he came to Palestine he was met by Jaddua, the High Priest, and later had the prophecies of Daniel read to him. Whether this is strictly true or otherwise, it is a fact that the Jews were treated well by Alexander and allowed religious freedom.

Following the death of Alexander, the Empire was divided into four by the leading Generals – Daniel 8:8 and 21-22. Ptolemy founded the Dynasty of the Ptolemies in Egypt – ended with the death of Cleopatra in 30 B.C. and the Roman Conquest of Egypt. Seleucis was the founder of the Seleucid Dynasty in Syria. Palestine became a buffer state between the Ptolemies of Egypt and the Seleucids of Syria. This period, may therefore, be sub-dived as follows:

A. Egyptian Period. 301-198 B.C. At first Palestine was dominated by Egypt. Within this period, under Ptolemy Philadelphus, the Greek translation of the Old Testament, known as the Septuagint, was begun in 285 B.C. and later became generally used by Greek speaking Jews – it was introduced into Palestine and by the time of our Lord was the Bible of the educated Jew. It is frequently quoted by New Testament writers.

B. Syrian Period. 198-167 B.C. The Seleucids finally attacked Palestine. Under Antiochus Epiphanes (meaning The Illustrious) Jerusalem was plundered in 170 B.C. and for three and a half years the Jews were deprived of religious and civil freedom – a small altar to Jupiter was erected on the altar of Burnt Offering and on the 25th of Chisleu (December) 168 B.C. a sow was offered on the Great Altar. The water in which part of the animal was boiled was sprinkled over copies of the law and every part of the Temple. There are those who consider this to be the fulfillment of the scripture in Daniel 9:27 and

11:31. No doubt it was a foreshadowing of the fulfillment of this scripture in days which are to come.

167-163. Independence.

III. THE RISE OF THE MACCABEES. 167-147 B.C.

Also known as the *Wars of the Jews*. Mattias, a Priest of Modiin and father of five sons, took his stand against apostates whom Antiochus had sent out to carry out idolatrous worship. He fled to the mountains and rallied a devoted band of men. After his death, his third son, Judas, succeeded him as leader of the Jewish forces in their fight for independence. Judas was known as Maccabees – that is, 'The Hammer' and the name is applied to the rest of the family. He regained possession of Jerusalem and the Temple which he cleansed and reinstituted worship on the same day as it had been polluted three years earlier. Thereafter this was commemorated annually in the feast known as the Feast of Dedication, which was kept for eight days – John 10:22. The struggle of the Maccabees continued for twenty years. Judas was killed in 161 B.C.

IV. THE RULE OF THE HASMONEAN PRIEST-KINGS. 146-63 B.C.

Judas Maccabees was succeeded by his brother, Jonathan, who became Priest and Ruler. Thus it was that the Priesthood became vested in the Hasmonean family. Jonathan was murdered in 143 B.C. and was succeeded by Simon, his brother, who finally overthrew the Syrian yoke. He was assassinated in 135 B.C. and was succeeded by his third son, John Hyrcanus. A period of freedom and independence followed. Samaria was mastered and John Hyrcanus destroyed the Samaritan Temple. He was succeeded by his son, Hyrcanus the Second, but his younger son, Aristopulus, assumed the rule. At this time Antipater was Governor of Idumea (Edom of the Old Testament which had been forcibly converted to Judaism under the reign of Hyrcanus the First). Antipater rallied to the cause of Hyrcanus the Second and called in the Roman General, Pompey, who defeated Aristopulus and reinstated Hyrcanus the Second – but henceforth Rome was to Rule.

V. ROMAN DOMINATION. 63-4 B.C.

Antipater of Idumea was the father of Herod. At first Herod had to flee to Rome, but later by his marriage to the granddaughter of Hyrcanus, he appeased the Jews and so the Herods (who were Edomites) entered the Jewish Hasmonean Dynasty and became the vassal rulers of Palestine under Rome.

In 37 B.C. Caesar Augustus confirmed Herod the Great (as he became known) as the Ruler of Provinces of Judah, Samaria, Galilee on the West of Jordan and Peraea and Idumea on the East. Herod sought to please the Jews by lavish schemes of building, likewise also the Samaritans. To remain in favor with Rome, he Romanized Cities and built Caesarea, naming it after Caesar Augustus. He commenced the reconstruction of the Temple in the 18th year of his reign – B.C. 20 – referred to in John 2:20.

Christ was born in B.C. 5 shortly before the death of Herod B.C. 4. Despite his lavish schemes, Herod was in fact a cruel tyrant – the massacre of Innocents being the particular piece of villainy for which he is chiefly remembered. He was succeeded by his son, Archelaus, who was later deposed by Publius Sulpitius Quirinius (the Greek name is used by Luke in his Gospel – Cyrenius). The President of Syria reduced Judea to a Roman Province to be governed by a Procurator. During Christ's ministry Judea and Samaria were governed by the Procurator, Pilate. Galilee was governed by Herod Antipas, the son of Herod the Great, with the title of Tetrarch. We read of Herod Antipas in the Gospels in connection with his unholy alliance with Herodias, and the beheading of John the Baptist. Christ also appeared before him – Luke 23:6-12.

II. THE DIVINE ORDERING OF WORLD EVENTS LEADING UP TO THE ADVENT OF CHRIST

In surveying the history of the 400 years prior to the birth of Christ there is apparent a Divine ordering of world events in preparation for the coming of Christ and the proclamation of the Gospel. In the rise and fall of Empires, it is seen how each one contributed in some measure and prepared the way for the coming of the Lord, so that in the very fullest possible way it is true that Christ came 'in the fullness of the time' – Galatians 4:4. The outstanding points to be noted are as follows:

A. LANGUAGE

Following the conquest of Alexander the Great, Greek traders and Greek culture had spread throughout the Mediterranean countries. A form of Greek had become the accepted international language of commerce throughout the known world and this language was used everywhere alongside of the local tongue. The name given to this form of Greek is 'koine dialektos', that is, 'common speech'. The common language of commercial intercourse considerably facilitated the spreading of the Gospel in the first century.

B. EASE OF COMMUNICATIONS – REMOVAL OF INTERNATIONAL BARRIERS

With the rise and rule of the Empire of Rome, international boundaries were removed and all Mediterranean countries were under the domination of Rome, so that it was possible to travel from one country to another more freely than in the present day of Passports and Visas. Wherever Rome went, Rome built roads, along which she could move her Legions speedily to quell any possible rebellion, so that not only were the international barriers removed, but there was considerable ease of travel. This contributed in no small measure to the evangelization of these countries in the first century. While Rome ruled there was also comparative peace.

C. THE DIASPORA

Is the name given to the Jews who had settled in the many centers of commerce in the Mediterranean area. They had done this following the growth of commerce under the Grecian Empire and also as a result of the persecution under Antiochus Epiphanes, so that in the first century there was in most of the principal cities a colony of Jews. It was to the Synagogues of these that Paul and other early missionaries of the Gospel went and first preached the Gospel. The Jews of the Dispersion became a starting point to evangelization in the City.

D. THE MESSIANIC HOPE OF THE JEWS

In the years preceding the birth of Christ there was a rising spirit of expectancy in the Jewish nation that their Messiah would come and deliver them. This spirit of expectancy arose chiefly from two reasons:

- The Traditions which had been added to the Law had become so numerous and complicated that common people found it quite impossible to either know or keep all that the Tradition of the elders demanded. People were looking for a new hope of salvation.

- The Conquest of the Land by Rome and the consequent oppression, heavy taxation and iron rule had caused the Jews to be eagerly looking for a deliverer.

E. WORLDWIDE DESIRE AND EXPECTANCY

The Jews were not the only people looking for One who was to come. Throughout the world there was a growing desire for a new order and for One to whom people could look as a leader in spiritual matters. This desire arose out of the following three causes:

- The prevailing Law and Debased Morals. With the passing of the culture of Greece there had been a steady decline in morality throughout the world, so that in the first century B.C. and the first Century A.D. morality was at its lowest ebb.

- The Futility of Idol Worship. People had come to realize the futility of the idolatrous practices and the worshipping of idols. Their gods had been unable to deliver them from Rome, and Rome had offered nothing spiritual.

- The Jews of the Dispersion had set up their Synagogues wherever they went and there they lived clean, moral lives and maintained their witness to Jehovah. It was undoubtedly their pure religion that helped to create the dissatisfaction with idols and also to reveal the low moral standards of the people to whom they went.

From the foregoing considerations, it will be seen that Christ came into a world which God had prepared in every way for the advent of the Lord Jesus.

III. HEBREW RELIGIOUS DEVELOPMENTS BETWEEN THE OLD AND NEW TESTAMENTS

In reading the Gospels it is at once apparent that there have been considerable changes in the religious life of the Jewish nation. Reference is made to certain forms of worship and sects, of which there is no mention in the Old Testament.

During the Babylonian exile no sacrifices were offered and the exiles gathered together to hear the scriptures read and to pray to Jehovah – Ezekiel 14:1 and 21 – so that the emphasis shifted from sacrifice to a veneration and keeping of the Law and subsequently to the growth of Traditions, that is, interpretations of the Law by the schools of Scribes. This led to worship in Synagogues.

SYNAGOGUES

The word means 'Assembly' or 'Gathering'. On the return of the exiles to Palestine, Synagogue worship continued. Every town and village had its Synagogue and at Jerusalem many Synagogues were built, and in the New Testament they are frequently mentioned. Wherever Jews went they established Synagogues for worship, and as has been mentioned earlier, these gave Paul his starting point in the majority of the Cities and towns visited in his missionary tours. It was the custom for the elders of the Synagogue to call upon visiting teachers or rabbis to read, pray and preach.

SANHEDRIN

This is also said to date from Ezra's time. It consisted of 70 or 72 chief Priests, Scribes, Elders or Princes of Israel and Heads of Families. It was the supreme governing body of the Jews. The Sanhedrin's power did, however, vary from time to time according to the ruling foreign power. In the times of our Lord, its power had been curtailed by Rome, and although it could pass sentence of death, power to confirm and execute the sentence rested with the Roman procurator – John 18:31.

APOCRYPHAL WRITINGS

The writings usually known as the Apocrypha were written during the 200 years before Christ. They consist of 14 books.

THE GROWTH OF SECTS

Sects or names of religious bodies never mentioned in the Old Testament are found in the New. The principal sects in the time of our Lord were as follows:

- Sadducees. The name was taken either from Zadok, the High Priest – I Kings 2:35 or because they claimed to be truly righteous ones – TSADDIKIM – who laid more stress on the moral than the ceremonial law. They refused to receive traditions or any development of divine truth except the law of Moses, thereby excluding that which was often implied in the Pentateuch. They refused to accept the supernatural – Acts 23:8 and were indifferent to the Messianic hope. Annas and his son-in-law, Caiaphas, were Sadducees. Sadducees were wealthy and occupied high positions in the Jewish nation. They were more bitter in their opposition to the early disciples than the Pharisees – because they preached Jesus and the resurrection – Acts 4:2.

- The Pharisees or Separatists – for that is the meaning of their name. They were separate from the common people. At the beginning they were a spiritual party and kept alive the Messianic hope. They accepted the Traditions of the Scribes and made it their business to keep the Traditions but became concerned chiefly with the outward performance and ignored the inner and deeper meaning of the Law. By reason of this, they were denounced by the Lord in the strongest possible terms – Matt. 23. Saul of Tarsus was a Pharisee, but after the Ascension of Christ they appear to have been less bitter in their opposition to the preaching of the Gospel. It will be recalled that Paul made his appeal to them in Acts 23:6.

- The Essenes – not actually referred to in the New Testament but a large Sect which arose as a reaction to the mechanical and Pharisaic form of religion. The adherents of Essenism lived a secluded life in lonely places and sought to realize true purity, but while venerating the Law, they rejected sacrificial offering. They also worshipped the sun and did not believe in the resurrection of the body but only in the immortality of the soul.

- The Herodians – they were chiefly a political party rather than a religious party, and comprised supporters and followers of the Herodian family. They were willing to sacrifice principle for worldly advantage and favor with Rome. Our Lord warned his followers to beware of the leaven of the Pharisees and of Herod; that is, falsehood that leads to hypocrisy and to compromise.

- The Galileans – these were originally the followers of Judas of Galilee and while similar to Pharisees in religious matters, taught that all foreign domination was contrary to God's will. The extremists of the Party were called Zealots. It would appear that one of the Apostles of the Lord was converted from this extreme sect - Matt. 10:4 and Luke 6:15.

- Proselytes – Matt. 23:15; Acts 2:10; 6:5; 13:43. These were Gentiles who obeyed the Law of Moses and offered sacrifices in the outer court. They were later divided into two groups:

Proselytes of Righteousness – not being well taught these only really exchanged their superstitious customs for an outward conformity to and an acceptance of the Jewish religion, thus lulling their conscience. They became bitter enemies of the Christian faith.

Proselytes of the Gate. These Gentiles had renounced idolatry and worship of God and knew of the promise of the Messiah. They are given various names in the New Testament, such as "They that feared God" "Worshippers" "Devout" – Acts 10:2; 16:14.

As might be anticipated, Christianity made considerable progress amongst them.

The Samaritans – These were the descendants from the colonists planted in the land by the Kings of Assyria after the ten tribes were taken captive – 2 Kings 17. When Zerubbabel and later Nehemiah returned to rebuild the Temple and the City of Jerusalem, the offer of the Samaritans to help was rejected and the enmity between the Samaritans and the Jews dated from that time and increased with the passing of the years. The Samaritans erected a Temple in Mt. Gerizim which was later destroyed by John Hyrcanus B.C. 109. The Samaritans accepted only the Pentateuch and rejected all other Jewish books. It will be recalled how our Lord went out of His way to meet the need of one Samaritan woman – John 4:4. It was amongst these people that Philip found such a good response – Acts 8:5-25.

The Jews of the Dispersion. Reference has already been made to these. Suffice it to say that they were divided into two groups; The Hebraists and the Hellenists.

The Hebraists clung tenaciously to the traditional Jewish ideas while the Hellenists imbibed much of the culture of Greece and a wider outlook on world affairs. Although the incident took place in Jerusalem it was because of the disputation between the Hellenists (rendered Crecians in Acts) and the Hebraists that the murmuring arose – Acts 6. Undoubtedly Paul meant that they belonged to the Hebraists when he said 'I am a Hebrew of the Hebrews' that is, one who had been brought up in the strict Jewish orthodox faith. In point of fact, he had also imbibed a Hellenistic outlook.

IV. THE LAND OF PALESTINE IN THE TIME OF OUR LORD

No longer is Palestine divided into a Southern and Northern kingdom as in the closing years of the historic section of the Old Testament. In the New Testament there are new divisions known as Judea, Samaria and Galilee on the West of Jordan, and Peraea and Decapolis on the East of Jordan.

The position of these areas and of all chief cities and places of particularly interest should be carefully noted on a map of Palestine in New Testament times.

JUDEA

A Roman province ruled by a Governor, known as a Procurator. For example, Pontius Pilate – Luke 3:1 : Matt. 27:2.

Places of outstanding interest:

Bethlehem – Birthplace of Christ.

Jerusalem – Mount of Olives,

Garden of Gethsemane and Calvary. Jericho. Bethany

SAMARIA

Judea and Samaria were ruled by the one Roman Procurator. Caesarea in Samaria was the normal place of residence for the Roman Governor, except at the Feasts, when he resided in Jerusalem. It was to Caesarea that Paul was taken – Acts 23:23-35. While Jews did not normally frequent Samaria, it was to the well of Sychar that Christ went to speak to the Samaritan woman, and to the City of Samaria Philip later went preaching the Gospel.

GALILEE

The inhabitants were zealous patriots, held in contempt by the Pharisees of the South. It was in Galilee that the Lord spent His childhood days and the years of His youth. A considerable portion of His ministry took place in Galilee.

Places of outstanding interest: Nazareth, Nain, Cana, the Sea of Galilee (also called the Sea of Tiberias).

Capernaum – a garrison town where Taxes were collected – Matt. 9:1 and 9. Here the Lord gave His discourse recorded in John 6.

Tiberias – where Herod Antipas had his palace, but of which we have no record of the Lord visiting.

Bethsaida – city of Andrew and Peter and Philip – John 1:44. Maybe also the city of John and James – Luke 5:10.

Chorazin – Matt. 11:20-24.

Magdala – on the West shore of the Sea of Galilee, and the probable home of Mary Magdalene.

PERAEA

The Jews from Galilee travelling to Jerusalem would avoid Samaria and hence cross over Jordan at the Ford at Bethabara in the North and back at the Ford opposite Jericho.

TETRARCHY OF PHILIP

Area occupied by the half tribe of Manasseh on the East of Jordan. Contained most of the area of Decapolis, meaning Ten Cities – Matt. 4:25.

Places of outstanding interest: Bethsaida Julias – Mark 6:34-45; 8:22-26. Caesarea Philippi – 8:27. Gergesa – Matt. 8:28. Gadara-Bethabara beyond Jordan – John 1:28; 10:40.

SYRIA

Apart from the incident in our Lord's childhood when He was taken down to Egypt, the only record of our Lord going beyond Palestine was to Tyre and Sidon in Syria – Matt. 15:21; Mark 7:24-31. There are those who believe Mt. Hermon in the Tetrarchy of Lysanias (Syria) to be the scene of the Transfiguration of Christ.

Damascus – the city to which Saul was travelling when he met the Lord Jesus and was converted.

Antioch – where as the result of the faithful preaching of the Gospel, many turned to the Lord – Acts 11: 19-30. From here, the Church first sent forth Paul and Barnabas – Acts 13.

GENESIS

Read the whole Book through carefully. Refer also to Joshua 1:1 and 7-8 and the exhortation to meditate on Genesis – Deuteronomy.

TITLE - In Hebrew Bible called 'Bereshith' – which is the first word meaning 'Beginning'.

'Genesis' – from Greek word meaning 'origin' or 'generation.'

No Book in the Bible has been more attacked by critics, so called scientists, infidels etc. Why? In many respects the most important Book of the Bible – impossible to think of the scriptures commencing with Joshua or even Exodus. Every great truth is here in germ – it has been called 'the seed plot of the Bible.' It is the Book that heralds the dawn of God's great redemptive purposes, leading on to the full light of God's complete revelation.

KEY WORD – Beginning
KEY TEXT – 1:1
KEY CHAPTER – 12

Genesis and Revelation have many points of likeness. Observe how the results of Genesis 3:1-7 are shown to be reversed in Revelation 21 and 22.

	GENESIS		REVELATION
3:23	Paradise closed	21:25	New paradise opened
3:24	Men cast out through sin	21:24	Man received in through divine grace
3:17	The curse imposed	22:5	The curse forever removed
3:24	Access to the Tree of Life barred	22:14	Access to the Tree of Life granted
3:16-19	Beginning of sorrow and death	21:4	End or removal of sorrow and death
3:6-7	A garden into which there came sin and defilement	21:27	A city into which nought that defileth shall ever enter in
3:19	Man's dominion broken and lost	22:3	Man's dominion restored through Christ, the new man
3:13	The Triumph of Satan	20:10	Ultimate and complete Triumph of the Lamb
3:8-10	God's walk with man interrupted	21:3	God walking and dwelling with man resumed.

That which began in Genesis is consummated in Revelation.

A garden	Becomes a city
One man	Becomes a race
Sin	Becomes fully manifested in the beast, the false prophet and the harlot
Physical death	Issues in the Second Death
Sentence passed on Satan	Becomes the Sentence Executed
The first Promise of a Triumphant Savior	Becomes final and complete fulfillment of the Promise

There are many New Testament references to characters and events and actual quotations from Genesis; e.g.

The Lord Jesus Christ referred to Adam and Eve becoming husband and wife – Matt. 19:4.

Abel – Matt. 23:35. Noah and the Flood – Luke 17:26-28. Abraham – John 8:56-58.

Judgment on Sodom – Luke 17:28-32.

Quotations from Genesis found in the New Testament:

Genesis 1:27	Matt. 19:4	Genesis 17:7	Gal. 3:16-19
" 2:2	Heb. 4:4	" 21:1-12	Heb. 11:18; Gal. 4:30
" 2:7	I Cor. 15:45	" 22:16-17	Heb. 6:13-14; James 2:23
" 12:3	Acts 3:25	" 25:23	Rom. 9:12
" 15:6	Rom. 4:3; James 2:23		

References to characters and events but not actual quotations:

Genesis 3:4-6	2 Cor. 11:3; I Tim. 2:14
" 3:6	Rom. 5:12-17
" 4:4	Heb. 11:4; Matt. 23:35
" 5:24	Heb. 11:5-6
" 14: 18-20	Heb. 7
" 19: 24-26	Luke 17:29-32; 2 Peter 2:6
" 22: 9	James 2:21
" 25: 3	Heb. 12:16
" 47:31	Heb. 11:21

Compare also Acts 7 which refers to events in Genesis.

The above references are not intended to be exhaustive.

Genesis records the Beginning of everything – but God!

1. The Universe	2. Mankind
3. Sin and Judgment in the world	4. The Promise of a Savior
5. Marriage and Family life	6. Birth and Death
7. Civilization	8. Arts, Crafts and industry
9. Languages and Nations	10. Israel the Chosen Race
11. War	12. Faith
13. Sacrifice	14. The Sabbath

Genesis contains the beginning of many important doctrinal truths.

The Trinity and Unity of God	Gen. 1:1-2, 26; 2:2
Composite Nature and Free Will of man	Gen. 1:26-27; 2:7; 2:16; 3:6
The Nature of Man's Sin and Sin's Penalty	Gen. 2:16; 3:1-6; 5:5, etc.
Atonement or Reconciliation through Blood	Gen. 4: 4
Justification by Faith – Abraham	Gen. 15:6
The Electing Grace of God – in choosing Seth, Noah, Shem, Abraham, Isaac, Jacob, Judah	Gen. 49:10; Psalm 78; Eph. 1:4
The True Nature of Satan and his Judgement	Gen. 3:4; Gen. 5; John 8:44

PRINCIPLE MESSAGE OF THE BOOK – Three-fold

- The Fall and Sin of man under every condition met by the Salvation of God.
- The Electing Grace of God
- The Divine Sovereignty in every Realm of Life.

STYLE AND STRUCTURE OF GENESIS: Prose, simple

Moses had a direct revelation from the Lord – Acts 7:37-38

The Book naturally divides into two main sections both

Historically	and	Doctrinally
Universal history Gen. 1-11		Generation Gen. 1:1 – 2:25
Patriarchal history Gen. 12-50		Degeneration Gen. 3:1 – 11:32
		Regeneration Gen. 12-50

In all three sections, Divine Sovereignty is manifest.

In four outstanding events Divine Sovereignty is manifest

In the natural realm	God created
In the human realm	God drove out the man from the garden
In the historic realm	Gad caused the judgment of the flood to come
In the international realm	God scattered the nations abroad upon the face of the earth

Divine Sovereignty is revealed in God's dealings with four men:

Abraham	Supernatural Call	
Isaac	Supernatural Birth	This presents a picture of God's dealing with His children now.
Jacob	Supernatural Care	
Joseph	Supernatural Guidance	

The author's plan of writing may be summed up by dividing the Book into eleven sections:

1. 'In the beginning' Gen. 1:1-2; 3	2. 'These are the generations of.. 2:4
3. …of Adam 5:1	4. …of Noah 6:9
5. …of sons of Noah 10:1	6. …of Shem 11:10
7. …of Terah 11:27	8. …of Ishmael 25:12
9. …of Isaac 25:19	10. …of Esau 36:1
11. …of Jacob 37: 2	

The Key verse Gen. 1:1 is not only a correct declaration of divine truth but also it answers false beliefs and infidelity by the following declarations:

	Genesis 1, 1
Atheism says 'there is no God'	… God
Polytheism says 'many Gods'	… God
Fatalism says 'life is chance, fate'	God created
Evolution says 'all evolved is evolving'	God created
Pantheism says 'God and Universe are identical'	God created heaven and earth
Materialism says 'matter is eternal'	God created heaven and earth

<u>The Outstanding Men of Faith</u>. Hebrews 11:1-16 gives divine commentary

Abel exhibits spiritual desire. Matt. 7:7 Enoch exhibits spiritual choice. Acts 16:31-34 Noah exhibits spiritual separation or renewal; i.e., speaking of regeneration. 2 Thess. 2:13-14	These three present a picture of steps into the Christian life.

The following four suggest aspects of the Christian life:

Abraham called to a life of faith Rom. 1:17; Gal. 3:11; 2 Cor. 5:7	Isaac (heir) called to a life of son-ship 1 John 3:1-2; Rom. 8:17
Jacob called to a life of service Rom. 12:1-2; Eph. 2:10	Joseph called to a life of suffering and ultimate glory 2 Cor. 1:5; 4:10, 17; 2 Tim. 2:12

Compare the faith of Abraham (always ready), Isaac, Jacob and Joseph.

Abraham reveals Active faith	Isaac reveals Passive faith
Jacob reveals Restless faith	Joseph reveals Persistent faith.

God is not ashamed to be called "their God." They are all different. God uses them all in His purpose. God is not limited by differences in people but by lack of obedience.

Types. See Romans 5:14. Hebrews 7:3; 9:8-9; 1 Cor. 10:4, 6 and 11.

Implied types – our Lord's reference to the manna – brazen serpent – Jonah. Divinely chosen illustration; person, event, thing, institution or ceremony.

The value of a type is:

- As an evidence of inspiration
- Enables us to recognize and understand more of the anti-type
- Illustrates truth, but not to build doctrine upon

Many Old Testament stories are analogies, rather than clearly defined types.

It may be as well to make the following observations before proceeding further regarding:

THE CREATION STORY – Gen. 2:4-25 is an amplification of 1:1 – 2:3. It is not a second different account but an enlargement expanding the essential details in the unfolding of God's plan and purpose – namely the creation and story of Adam. This method is in accordance with the method used throughout the Book.

THE DAYS OF CREATION – 1:1 declares God's creative act. In 1:2 the Hebrew verb translated "was" is "became" in 2:7. It is generally translated "became" or "it came to pass" in the O.T. It is especially declared in Isaiah 45:18 – God did not create the world "in vain," the same Hebrew word as "without form." The double expression "without form and void" only occurs elsewhere in Isaiah 34:11 and Jeremiah 4:23 – both passages dealing with results of divine judgment. If this is correct interpretation, the cause of the Judgment resulting in the chaos of 1:2 not specifically stated. It may have had to do with rebellion and fall of Satan as indicated in Isaiah 14.

Job 38:4-7 angels shouted for joy. 2 Pet. 2:11; 2 Thess. 1:7; Psa. 103:20; Eph. 6:12; Heb. 1:13-14 angels servants. 2 Pet. 2:4; Matt. 25: 41 fallen angels.

Two named angels: Michael – Jude 9. Gabriel – Dan. 10:73; Luke 1:19

Lucifer (morning star) – Isa. 14:9-17, vs. 12; Ezek. 28:12-18. Prince of world. John 12:31; Eph. 2:2;

2 Cor. 4:4; John 14:30; Matt. 4:9; 25:41; Isa. 14:12; Luke 10:18.

Note also the use of the word "creation" in 1:1; 1:21; 1:27- it is only applied to original creation, animals and men. It is not used of the earth itself in the six days – the difference seems to be emphasized in 2:3.

It does therefore seem to suggest the creation is referred to in 1:1 and that from 1:2 onwards it is the account of reconstruction with special reference to creation of animals and man. Ex. 20:11 – 24 hour-days – 6 days of creation.

There are other interpretations such as:

- Six days of creation of 24 hours each
- Six days were ages of undefined length
- Six days of revelation granted to Moses
- Six tablets from which he took his record

There is no doubt whatsoever about the fact that in the beginning God created the Universe and also that Man was the subject of a special creative act.

THE FLOOD – testified to by universal tradition and 20th Century archaeology. There is no doubt whatsoever that the flood was a historic event. The question that arises is – was it a universal flood? Whatever answer we may give to that, one thing is absolutely certain, it achieved the purpose God had in mind – see 7:21-24; Matt. 24:37-39 . 3-17 billion years – age of earth.

THE SPIRITUAL AND TYPICAL TEACHING OF THE BOOK

I. The Ministry of the Holy Spirit revealed Chap. 1:2. Note the word "moved.' Also "fluttering" – Deut. 32:11; Luke 3:22. The Holy Spirit is seen brooding over the state of chaos and darkness, even as now He broods over the darkened soul, brings to life and gently leads the believer on – 1 Pet. 1:2; John 1:32-33; 2 Thess. 2:13; 1 Pet. 1:23-25.

II. The Sun – Moon – Stars 1:14-18, as types of the Lord Jesus – the Church – Saints

Psa. 136:7-8; Jer. 31:35. The sun and moon are referred to as light givers.

The great Light-giver. Mal. 4:2; Psa. 27:1. Who is the Light giver? John 1:4-9; 8:12; 9:5 and 3:19-20 where reference is made to the rejection of the light. Think of all that the sun does. It provides a picture of the ministry of the Lord Jesus, either life giving or scorching – 2 Cor. 2:16. The greater light rules the day. We note from many passages that we are at present in the night and the day of Christ's rule is yet to come. Rom. 13:11-12; 1 Thess. 5:5-8; 2 Thess. 2:2. Eclipse – another body between moon and sun. Moon symbolic of believers – no light of our own.

The lesser Light-giver has no light of its own – reflects the glory of the sun. Prov. 4:18; Matt. 5:14 & 16; Eph. 5:8-14; Phil. 2:14-16. The lesser light is 'to rule the night' – not to be subject to it! Rom. 5:17; 8, 37.

The Stars – Psa. 147:4; Dan. 12:3; Gen. 15:5 compared with Heb. 11:12.

III. The Creation and Purpose of Man – 1:27-28 (nature); 2:7-8 & 15 (location).

Nature: spirit, soul and body

Spirit – God-conscious

Soul – self-conscious

Body – spirit and soul become world conscious 1 Tim. 2:13; Eph. 5:28-33

- To be in the likeness of God – godlike – godly has mind and will
- To have dominion on the earth – reign as a king – kingly
- To serve the Lord God in His garden – to render service/a worker serving.

What is the purpose of God's new creation in man?

- Rom. 8:28-29; Phil. 3:21; 1 Cor. 15:49; 2 Cor. 3:18; 1 John 3:2
- Rom. 6:14; 5:17; Rev. 1:5-6; 5:10

- John 20:22. The Lord breathed on His disciples to impart His Spirit and thus equip for service – 'a bond slave' – 1 Cor. 3:9 (his choice to serve). Rev. 22:3-5; Rom. 5:20b

IV. Adam – a Type of Christ – Rom. 5:12-19 – particularly v. 14; 1 Cor. 15:45-50.

   A. As Head of the Race – The First Man – the Representative Man, his seed not only inheriting his nature but bound by his actions – sharers in the fruit thereof.

   Gen. 5:1-3; Romans 5:12 and 19; 1 Cor. 15:48-49.

   The Last Adam is the Second Man – the Lord from heaven, 1 Cor. 15:47.

   He is the Head of the New Race – the Representative Man.

   In Christ we become sharers of His divine nature – 2 Peter 1:4 and are also bound by His actions and sharers in the fruits of all that He has done.

By natural birth -	By new birth -
i.e. Generation	i.e. Regeneration
- in Adam	- in Christ
physical, human life	spiritual life
partakers of Adam's sinful nature	partakers of the Divine, holy nature
sharers of Adam's action	sharers in Christ's death
and fruit thereof	resurrection and in the fruit thereof.

   B. Adam's characteristics portray Christ.

As a Man	A Servant	A King	A Husband
Gen. 1:26-27 - 2:4	Gen. 2:15; Phil. 2:7	Gen. 1:26; 2:19-20	Gen. 2:20-25; Rev. 21:2
Phil. 2:7-8	Isa. 42:1; Matt. 20:28	John 19:19; Rev. 19:16	Eph. 5:25; 5:23-32
	Mark 10:45		
Luke	Mark	Matthew	John

C. As the Founder and Husband of His Bride – Gen. 2:21-24. Read carefully Eph. 5:23-32

V. The Fall of Man and the Outcome – 3:1-24. A historic event.

A. The temptation permitted. Man with free will must have the opportunity to exercise his will – no compulsion to sin – satisfied and enjoying unbroken fellowship with God.

B. Satan's approach – was to the woman – 1 Tim. 2:14; 2 Cor. 11:3; that is, through that which Adam loved. Eve was beguiled; Adam went into sin by clear choice.

C. Satan's method:

- God's Word Discredited and doubt cast upon it – 3:1
- God's Word Denied – 3:3
- God's Character Defamed – 3:5

Spiritual evil took physical form to induce spiritual man through physical side of his makeup.

D. The nature of temptation: v 5 – self realization, assert your right, please yourself – even if it is contrary to God's Word. Isa. 14:14

E. The appeal of the temptation: 3:6 – note 1 John 2:16.

- "Tree good for food" – lust of the flesh – Matt. 4:3
- "It was pleasant to the eye" – lust of the eyes – Matt. 4:5. Bodily senses.
- "To be desired to make one wise" – pride of life – Matt. 4:8. James 1:14-15 - Intellect.

F. The immediate outcome of the Fall: three-fold as far as man is concerned.

Their glory departed and there was a sense of shame. Compare Rom. 8:3 with Luke 9:29 and 32. Contrast Phil. 3:21.

The fulfillment of 2:17 in spiritual realm – to be later dead to God followed by physical death as proof of the fruit of sin.

They desired to get away from God – conscious of barrier between, 3:8 and 3:10.

G. God's first call to fallen man – 3:9. Where art thou? Rom. 5:6-8; 1 John 4:10 and 19.

God, not man, makes the first approach.

H. God's first promise of the Redeemer – 3:15. Emphasizing the Deliverer was to be the seed of the woman – fulfilled in Virgin Birth.

"He shall bruise...thou shalt bruise..." fulfilled in the Cross. Head – destroyed/incurable. Heel – incapacitated.

I. The curse pronounced upon the earth – 3:17.

The only crown this world could offer Christ was the evidence and fruit of sin – John 19:2

J. The purpose of the first sacrifice – 3:21. To meet and cover man's need.

VI. The Offerings of Cain and Abel – 4:1-15; Heb. 11:4 : 1 John 3:12; Jude 11.

Reveals the two methods of approach to God – Man's way and God's way. The method reveals attitude of heart.

Abel's offering was by faith. Compare Rom. 10:17. Cain's offering was as he pleased – proved by no desire to remedy his way when God spoke to him 4:6-7; Rom. 10:3.

Compare Luke 18:10-14. Parable of Pharisee and publican.

The enmity of the two seeds is seen (foreshadowed in 3:15) – stated in 1 John 3:12. Sin always causes conflict between God and man and man and man.

VII. The Translation of Enoch – 5:22-24; Heb. 11:5

A type of the rapture or translation of the saints – 1 Thess. 4:17

Enoch in patriarchal order – Elisha in prophetic order and ascension of the Lord all seem to indicate the coming translation of the saints.

This is significant in view of the main theme of Enoch's preaching – Jude 14-15.

VIII. Methuselah's long life – 5:27.

Demonstrates God's forbearance – 2 Peter 3:9. Methuselah means "when he dies it shall come to pass." A computation of Methuselah's age reveals that he died in the year when Noah was 600 years old, that is, the year of the flood. Enoch named his son Methuselah. Enoch preached the coming of the flood which came to pass when his son Methuselah died.

IX. The Flood – 6:1-8, 21

The essential fact is stated in chapter 7:21-23; Matt. 24:36-39

An act of judgment for sin of the vilest type, violating and destroying the physical frame of mankind, yet in it all God's graciousness seemed to be triumphant – v. 8. God is seen to be fulfilling His purposes and preserving the way of redemption and regeneration for men. Compare Genesis 6:8 "By grace" with Heb. 11:7 "By faith" – Eph. 2:8. How did Noah come to know – Genesis 6:9 and 13 and Psalm 25:14. In N.T. Sons of God means us. O.T. Sons of God means angelic beings Job 1:6; 2:1. Hosea 1:10.

Noah – obeyed - built – preached – 2 Peter 2:5. How foolish it must have seemed – 1 Cor. 1:27-28 and 4:9-10. Noah means rest.

A type of individual believers and of the Church being taken out of judgment and brought into a new world.

"ark" symbolic of Christ – they were shut in but could tumble about inside.

Observe that the Lord "shut in" those who were in the Ark – Isa. 32:2. 2 lines of thought: Were the men of old fallen angels (the ones who corrupted the tribes) or was it the sinful line of Seth?

X. The Babel dispersion – 11.

Estimated to have taken place 300 years after the flood. Contrast 11:4 to 9:1 and 7 which contain God's command to Noah. It is seen that at Babel man is uniting in opposition and rebellion against God. It was a religious project – a man-made answer to God – a place of idolatrous worship. The judgment was two-fold:

Confusion of language – v. 9. The difference of original languages vast and unexplained except by this record. Contrast with the true unity of Acts 2:6-11. Original languages show not a gradual difference, but a cataclysmic difference, such as is to be expected from the judgment of Babel.

Scattered – v. 8-9. Compare Gen. 11:10-19 and 10:25. Peleg born 101 years after the flood – lived 239 years. Babel mans "confusion." Note future reference in the Bible to Babylon which opposes and takes captive the people of God until its final reference in Revelation. Babylon ("mystery of iniquity" in Rev. seeks to persecute the saints).

XI. The Call and Obedience of Abraham – 12. Rom. 4:1-3 and 16-25; Gal. 2:6; James 2:23.

The principle of blessing is stated verse 2; 1 Peter 2:9; Eph. 1:3 and 6 and 12; 1 Cor. 15:58. The promise and revelation granted to Abraham is progressive – 12:2; 13:16; 15:4-5; 22:17-18.

The chapters on Abraham need careful and thoughtful study and will yield much spiritual truth. Contrast his response to God with the attitude of Lot. The two men reveal two modes of Christian living – the one spiritual and the other carnal.

XII. Abraham offering up Isaac – 22.

A picture of the great sacrifice of Calvary – Heb. 11:17.

XIII. Melchizedek – the Priest and King – 14:17-22; Heb. 6:19 – 7:1-28, especially noting 7:3.

The writer to the Hebrews specifically refers to Melchizedek as a type of Christ. Is. 32:1; 9:6-7; Zech. 6:13.

XIV. The Choosing of Isaac's wife – 24

Why such a wealth of detail of this incident? An analogy of the calling of the Church to be the Bride of Christ through the work of the Holy Spirit.

Abraham sent his unnamed servant to woo a bride for his dearly beloved, his only son, Isaac.

The bride must be prepared to forsake her old life and family for another she has never seen – verses 4-8; 1 Peter 1:8. The servant goes forth from the father's house – v. 10; Acts 2:33 – and reveals something of the wealth and treasure of his master's household.

XV. Jacob's ladder – 28:12-17

A picture of the one who was to come out of Jacob and cause blessing to come to all the families of the earth – John 1:51.

XVI. Joseph – a type of the Lord Jesus – 37:1 onwards

There are said to be 137 likenesses between Joseph and the Lord Jesus Christ. How many can you note?

XVII. The Prophetic utterance of 49:9-10 should be specially noted – Rev. 5:5; Luke 1:32

XVIII. The Angel of Jehovah – is a reference to pre-incarnation appearances of Christ, called Christophanies.

To Hagar – 16:7-14. To Abraham – 18:19 and 22. To Jacob – 31:11-13, 32 at Peniel.

The Book opens with the glory of God manifest in creation and man made in His image in a garden, a sanctuary, and ends with "a coffin in Egypt." (Joseph) It is the story of man's sin and failure, but with the promise and foreshadowing of God's intervention.

The remainder of the Bible is a revelation of God's plan and promise being fulfilled until man is again in the likeness of God, in the sanctuary of God. Rev. 22:1-21.

"He which testifieth these things saith, 'Surely I come quickly.' Amen. Even so, come, Lord Jesus."

EXODUS

Read the whole Book, taking special note of the contents of chapter 12 (Passover). Read also Acts 7:17-44 and 1 Cor. 10:1-13

TITLE – Exodus comes from the Greek and means 'Way Out' or 'departure.' It is the word used in Luke 9:31. The name in Hebrew Bible is 'We-elleth Shemoth' – 'These are the Names' or 'Shemoth' – 'Names.' 2 Pet. 1:15

KEY WORD – Redemption

KEY VERSES – 3:8 and 12:13 and 23

KEY CHAPTER – Exodus 12 – the Institution of the Passover. Hence, the Outstanding Presentation of Christ in this Book is as THE PASSOVER LAMB. Chap. 2 - 12 - 80 years. 12 – end – one year.

HISTORIC PERIOD – It is difficult to be certain of the period covered in chapter 1. From birth of Moses, chapter 2, to the end of chapter 12 is just over 80 years. From the Exodus to the setting up of the tabernacle, that is chapters 12 to 40, is one year. The date of the Exodus of the Children of Israel from Egypt is usually considered to be 1400 B.C.

SUMMARY OF THE CONTENTS OF THE BOOK – The Book may be divided in several ways. Two natural divisions are:

    A. Historical – Ex. 1 to 18 – This section contains the history of the Sons of Jacob becoming a nation and in bondage in Egypt. The birth and training of Moses. His flight from and return to Egypt. The judgment of the plagues upon the Egyptians, the institution of the Passover for the Children of Israel and the account of their coming out of Egypt.

B. Legislative – Ex. 19 to 40 – This section deals with the giving of the Law. The appointment of Aaron and the Aaronic priesthood, the ritual worship and details of the construction of the tabernacle and its furniture.

The following is a fuller Summary based on the main movements of the Book as indicated by the words on the right:

1. The Children of Israel in Bondage	1:1 to 2:25	Bondage
2. The Call of Moses, the man of God	3:1 to 4:31	Call
3. The Judgment upon the Egyptians	5:1 to 11:10	Judgment
4. The Institution of the Passover	12:1-51	Passover
5. The Deliverance of the Children of Israel	13:1 to 19:2	Deliverance
6. The Revelation of God's Will for His People	19:3 to 40:38	Revelation
The Unfolding of God's will	20 to 24	Will of God
The Way of Approach to God made clear	25 to 40	Way of God

In this Book there is clearly revealed the Power of God, the Holiness of God and the Wisdom of God, so that a summary which would convey this three-fold message of the Book would be as follows:

Divine Power manifest in the Exodus	1 to 18
Divine Holiness manifest in the Law	19 to 24
Divine Wisdom manifest in the Tabernacle	24 to 40

THE OUTSTANDING CHARACTERS – Moses, the man of God – Read all you can of him, not only in this book but elsewhere in scripture. In Particular note his Songs of Psalm – Exodus 15:1-19; Deuteronomy 31:30 to 32:43 (compare Rev. 15:30); Psalm 90. Note the threefold division of his life given by Stephen in Acts 7:20-44.

Moses lived in own strength	Acts 7:23
Moses learned in weakness – 40 years in the wilderness	Acts 7:30
Moses proving God's strength through his weakness	Acts 7:36

This book contains the Outstanding Miracle of the Old Testament – the bringing of the Children of Israel out of Egypt through the Red Sea.

COMPARISON BETWEEN GENESIS AND EXODUS – It is profitable to note the relationship between the five Books of the Pentateuch to each other in a progressive sequence.

IN GENESIS	IN EXODUS
The Story of man's sin, failure and need – man's need	The story of redemption and way of deliverance – God's provision for the need
The electing grace of God is revealed	The manner by which election becomes operative; namely, through the shedding of blood and the obedience of faith.
God chooses a People for Himself	God redeems and calls out a People for Himself

In the early part of the Book two important truths are revealed and illustrated:

- The Manner of God's Working in Human History – Sovereign and Providential – encompassing national life – Egypt, and yet interwoven with the smallest details of personal life – Moses.

- The Responsibility of Man – man is not absolved from the responsibility of personal choice leading to destiny. National responsibility also illustrated as in the case of Israel and Egypt. Heb. 11:24.

SPIRITUAL AND TYPICAL TEACHING OF THE BOOK

I. The Exodus of the Children of Israel from Egypt is one of the important movements in human history. The event is also a parable of history in that it sets forth the need and deliverance of a soul. Observe the following steps:

- In bondage
- Conscious of need
- Crying for deliverance
- Pharaoh seeking to retain hold – reminding of the fight against spiritual wickedness and the evil one
- Redemption and deliverance through the death of a lamb
- Resulting in a guided life
- The life miraculously provided for
- The Word or Law given by which the people of God were to order their lives

The Exodus brought to Israel:

		In Christ the believer finds:
New Life	Ex. 12:2	John 10:27-28
Liberty	Ex. 13:3	Gal. 5:1
Fellowship	Ex. 12 to 14	1 John 1:3
Assurance	Ex. 6:7-8	1 John 5:13; John 17:3,20-21; 2 Peter 1:4

From the Book of Exodus, the Christian life may be summed up as – Separation Salvation Singing

II. The Angel of the Lord. Ex. 3. The Burning Bush!

A little common thorn bush, ablaze with the glory of God – an Acacia, from which the Shittim wood is obtained and which was used in the tabernacle. A picture and a foreshadowing of the incarnation of Christ.

John 1:1 and 14; 1 John 1:1-2

"I am THAT I am" – compare references in John's Gospel – "I am.."

III. The Hardening of Pharaoh's heart.

Necessary to recognize that Pharaoh was a wicked man, already pursuing a course of evil and oppression to the people of God. An outcome of the deceitfulness of sin is that it leads to the hardening of the heart and a strengthening of the will against God.

Read the following references (preferably in R.V.) referring to Pharaoh hardening his heart – 7:13,14,22 ; 8:15,19,32; 9:7 prior to 9:12 where it says, "The Lord hardened the heart of Pharaoh." (Although it had been predicted – 4:21 and 7:3). Other references to Pharaoh hardening his heart – 9:34-35; 13:15 – R.V. margin. Three different Hebrew words are used with varying shades of meaning. Those verses which are underlined in the above references each contain the word which could equally be rendered 'was dull' or 'heavy', that is, insensible to the voice of God. It will also be seen that Pharaoh hardened his heart immediately after the miracles of the plagues.

Romans 1:24,26,28 are an apt commentary on the above. When human choice has been exercised finally, then God seals the choice of the human will.

Pharaoh is seen as a type of the adversary, in opposition to the people of God.

IV. The Ten Plagues – Ex. 7 to 12

The significance of the plagues was that each of these was aimed at the gods the Egyptians worshipped.

- The river Nile turned to blood. 7:14-25. The Nile was worshipped as the source of life in Egypt.
- The Frogs. 8:1-5. The Goddess Hekt had a frog head.
- Lice from the sacred dust. 8:16-19. Seb, the earth god.

- Beetles or Sand Flies. 8:20-32. The sacred scarabs of Beelzebub were beetles or sand flies.

- Murrain. 9:1-7. The contagious fever on cattle, affecting even their bulls. The sacred Bull, Apis.

- Boils. 9:8-12. Ashes were taken from the sacrifices offered to Typhon and scattered in the air to produce blessing. Now by acts of Moses: 9:8-12, the ashes produced boils.

- Hail and Fire. 9:13-35. Shu, god of the atmosphere.

- Locusts. 10:4. Attack on Serapis the protector from locusts.

- Darkness. 10:21-29. Attack on Ra, the Sun god.

- Death of Firstborn. 1:1 - 12:36. No god able to withstand against God, not even Pharaoh (and his son) who were worshipped as gods.

V. Moses's stand against Pharaoh – Ex. 8 – 10

Teaches that the man of faith can never compromise. Man's faith must express itself in worship, submission and absolute obedience to the uttermost, even in the face of opposition. 2 Cor. 6:17-18 and 7:1.

VI. The Passover Lamb – a type of Christ – Ex. 12

Make a careful note of the points of comparison.

v. 5 Lamb, first born and without blemish.

John 1:29; 1 Peter 1:18-19; Luke 2:7; Col. 1:15

John 8:46; Heb. 7:26; 2 Cor. 5:21

v. 6 Lamb to be slain. 1 Cor. 2:2; Rev. 5:6

v. 7 Blood to be shed and applied or sprinkled. 1 Pet. 1:2

v. 46 No bone to be broken. John 19:33 and 36

v. 3 & 30 In every home in land, one was dead, no neutral home, either the firstborn or the lamb. Rom. 5:8 and 6:23

v. 2 Israelites were to reckon their life as a nation from the day of the Passover. John 3:7; Gal. 4:3-6

Ch. 13:2 All the firstborn redeemed by blood were to be set apart – 1 Cor. 6:19-20

The blood of the Lamb made them Safe, trusting God's promise made them Sure – Salvation and Assurance.

VII. The Children of Israel's Deliverance from Pharaoh and Egypt – Ex. 14

There are other instances on record of the wind driving back the waters of lakes and seas, but it must be recognized that this event was God's direct intervention to bring Salvation to His people. It is the standard miracle of the Old Testament – Ex. 14:22; Micah 7:15.

It reveals God's

Judgment – on Egyptians; Grace to the Israelites

Power - A way through the Red Sea; Provision – Manna and water in the wilderness

Guidance – Pillar of cloud and of fire; Faithfulness – the promise to Abraham honored

VIII. The Manna – Bread from Heaven – Ex. 16:4, 14-21.

A type of the Lord Jesus – particularly of His incarnation and life here below, in coming down from Heaven. John 6:48, 51, 63.

IX. The Smitten Rock and Gushing Water – Ex. 17:1-7

This is a striking picture of Calvary followed by Pentecost – 1 Cor. 10:4; John 4:13-14; 7:37-39

God cleft the Rock – Is. 53:10. Note also Num. 20:7-12; Heb. 9:26 and 28; 10:10, 12, 14

X. Moses' Intercession on the Mount and Joshua fighting in the Valley – Ex. 17:8-16

Faith and Fighting	Prayer and Practice
Rom. 8:34; Eph. 6:17-18	Heb. 7:25; 1 Tim. 6:12

Our victory depends upon His intercession.

XI. Moses and the Giving of the Law

It is important to remember that at first Moses was rejected, later becoming Israel's Deliverer from bondage, and then gave the Law by which people were to live. Ex. 2:14,19,25; Acts 7:35; 1 Cor. 10:1-2

So Christ rejected and yet becoming Savior gives His new Law for Christian conduct, contained in the Epistles – Rom. 13:10. It will be observed that the Law in Ex. 20 commences with the commandment to be right with God. Compare Matt. 22:36-40; Mark 10:17-22; 12:28-34.

XII. The Tabernacle

Speaks to us of Christ. The Tabernacles is a study in itself and is not covered by these notes.

XIII. Aaron – The Great High Priest

Aaron was taken from among the Children of Israel – 28:1. He was to be clothed with holy garments, to be distinguished from among the people. Christ, through man, is distinguished, 'horizoned', 'marked out' from among men by His holy character and resurrection. Rom. 1:3-4; Heb. 4:14-15; 5:1-4.

The Garments of the High Priest as described in Ex. 28 and 39 are full of typical meaning.

LEVITICUS

Read the whole book particularly noting Lev. 16 and 26; 1 John 1:7-9; 1 Peter 1:14-16.

The Epistle to the Hebrews should also be read in conjunction with Leviticus.

TITLE - The name Leviticus comes from the Greek and means "Pertaining to the Levites" – actually Levites only mentioned in Lev. 25:32-33. Hebrew name 'Va-yich-rah' meaning 'and He called.' This book is God's call to His redeemed people to be holy and to hold communion with Him.

KEY WORDS – 'Holiness' and 'communion'; 'Holy' 87 times, 'Atonement' 45 times.

KEY VERSES – Lev. 11:44-45; 16:30 and 17:11; 19:2

HISTORIC PERIOD

Just over one month corresponding with the 1st April when the Tabernacles was set up – Ex. 40:2, 17 and Lev. 1:1 – and 20th May when they departed from Mount Sinai – Num. 10:11. One of the most remarkable books of the Old Testament by reason of its short time span.

OUTSTANDING CHARACTERISTICS

A book of ritual not history. 56 times we read "The Lord spoke….. said….commanded." Lev. 1:1, etc. Thus nearly all the words claimed to have been spoken by God to Moses "out of the tabernacle." Therefore, it should receive very special attention – in practice one of the most neglected books of the Bible. The reason for this is possibly two-fold:

- Considered to be too ritualistic and symbolic to be understood, or

- Considered not worthy of attention as the ritual has now passed away. The spiritual truths taught, however, abide.

CENTRAL CHAPTERS - Lev. 16 – the Atonement chapter and Lev. 26 – the Blessing and Cursing chapter.

CHIEF CHARACTERS - Moses and Aaron, the High Priest

Aaron – A High Priest is appointed for a people already redeemed – he only acted as intercessor for Israel. Likewise Christ is only a High Priest for believers – the Church – John 17:2; Rom. 8:34; Heb. 7:25. There is no priesthood for the unbelieving world. To unbelievers, Christ will be the Judge.

SUMMARY OF THE BOOK

Dividing the Book into two Divisions

1. Sacrifice – the Basis of fellowship Lev. 1 – 17. Cleansing by the shedding of blood is shown to be the foundation of fellowship. Reference is made to the offerings. Lev. 1-7, the priesthood Lev. 8-10, the people Lev. 11-16 and the altar Lev. 17.

2. Separation – the Walk of fellowship Lev. 18-27. Walking in the light is shown to be the condition of fellowship. Regulations are given concerning the people Lev. 18-20, the priests Lev. 21-22, the feasts of the Lord Lev. 23-24 and coming occupation of the land (Canaan) Lev. 25-27.

Within this section, the phrase "I am Lord" occurs nearly 50 times. We might term these two sections:

	Christ's work
Positional Truth (our standing)	For us
Practical Truth (or application)	In us

The Message of the Book

In relation to Exodus:

In Exodus	In Leviticus
A people are redeemed and brought nigh to God	It is shown how the people may be kept nigh to God
The people are delivered from a sinful Egypt	They are called to walk in purity of life
God's approach to man	Man's approach to God
Christ as Savior	Christ as Sanctifier
God is love	God is light

Leviticus stands in the same relation to Exodus as the Epistles are to the Gospels.

In Exodus, the Lord redeems Gospels

In Leviticus, He dwells in the midst Epistles

Genesis – Man ruined by sin

Exodus – Man redeemed by God (Christ as Savior)

Leviticus – man restored to communion and fellowship with God (sanctified)

The Outstanding Message of the whole narrative is the Holiness of God. Ex. 15:11; Lev. 19:2; 20:7.

In setting forth the holiness of God, it is necessary to awaken sense of sin and thus prepare for the coming of Christ of which the Tabernacle and Sacrifice is spoken. Importance to realize God's character is unchanged, unchanging – Levitical priesthood and sacrifice may have passed away but the spiritual realities which they declare abide for all time. The idea of atonement through propitiatory sacrifice is belittled today – hence the need to heed the message of Leviticus.

This message is declared in a twofold way with a third logical and necessary outcome:

1. The defiling nature of sin is revealed – the book calls for constant shedding of blood, sacrifice and offering – thus declaring that the nature of sin is such that sinful man cannot approach a Holy God except on the basis of atonement through the shedding of blood. Lev. 17:11; Heb. 9:22.

   Continual sacrifice and ever-glowing fires are intended to burn into heart and mind and consciences of the people their deep sinfulness.

2. God's remedy revealed. It is possible, if sin is confessed, not only to approach God but to have continual access to Him.

   The Levitical sacrifices were only temporary and as such had to be constantly repeated, thus pointing to the coming perfect sacrifice of Christ at Calvary once in the end of the world. Heb. 7:27; 9:26-28.

3. The book deals with bodily cleanness, moral law and hygienic precautions for everyday life. The people made holy by redemption are called to lead holy lives. True holiness has its root in personal, social and national life. Lev. 11:44-46; 19:2.

SPIRITUAL AND TYPICAL TEACHING

Leviticus has been called "A treasury of divinely chosen illustrations."

Five principal offerings:

A. Burnt Offering – Lev. 1 Wholly burnt and completely offered to God. v. 9, 13, 17. The offering was a sweet smelling savor unto the Lord. Eph. 5:2	Godward

B. Meal (or cereal) S.R.V.) Offering – Lev. 2 A handful, memorial burn – greater part kept back for the sustenance of the priest. Fine flour mixed with oil. Isa. 53, 10a. Holy Spirit supplies and sustains and meets need of man. Acts 4:32-35; Phil. 2:17	Manward
C. Peace Offering – Lev. 3 Fat and certain other parts offered. Remainder for priest. Perfect fellowship and friendship. God at peace with man and man at peace with God. Rom. 5:1; John 16:33; Eph. 2:13-19; Col. 1:20-21	Godward and Manward
D. Sin Offering – Lev. 4 For specific sin against God's commandments. Laying hands on the victim and then slain and offered. Fat burnt on altar and all remainder burnt outside the camp. Heb. 13: 12-13; 2 Cor. 5:20-21; Gal. 2:20; 5:24; 6:13 Reconciliation, restored relationship.	Godward
E. Trespass Offering – Lev. 5 For trespass or defilement, principally in relation between man and men. Eph. 2:14; John 10:16, 18. The sacrifice of Calvary enables man to live in right relationship with God and with fellow man.	Manward

The Consecration of Priests – Lev. 8

The High Priest Cleansed v. 6, Clothed v. 7-8, Crowned v. 9, Anointed v. 12. Note the anointing was before the sacrifice. A type of Christ. The sons of Aaron who were priests were Cleansed v. 6, Clothes v. 13, Anointed or Crowned with oil v. 30 (21:12) and Charged or Instructed v. 35. These are a type of believers and true to type they were anointed after the sacrifice.

The priests have a double identification with the sacrifice:

- The laying on hands, v. 14, one with the sacrifice,
- Sprinkled with the blood, v. 22-24, cleansed by the sacrifice.

1 John 1:7-9 concerning sin 1 Pet. 1:14-16

Sacrifice – entails shedding of blood

Oblation – doesn't entail shedding of blood (such as meal)

Offering – general term – can mean both.

OFFERINGS

	Of Christ	Of Believer
A. Burnt Godward	The Son of God wholly devoted to the will of God	Rom. 12:1. A life wholly yielded to God
B. Meal (cereal) Manward	The perfect man – meeting every human need	Sacrificed service for others
C. Peace Godward and Manward	The mediator restoring broken relationship	Service to God and fellowship with believers
D. Sin Godward	The Sin Bearer	Identification with Christ
E. Trespass Manward	Bearing and thus removing sin	Dead to Sin

In the case of our Lord this double identification signifies our Lord is both the sacrifice and the High Priest.

In the case of the believers they are both identified with the death of Christ and they are cleansed by it.

It is after the sacrifice that both the High Priest and Priests are anointed together v. 30 – there is full identification in the priestly office. Heb. 2:11.

The application of the blood to the priest, v. 24, signified ears sanctified to hear the word of the Lord – hands sanctified to serve the Lord – feet sanctified to walk in the ways of the Lord.

The Judgment of Nadab and Abihu – Lev. 10

There is only one way of approach to God. John 14:6

Foods which May and May Not be Eaten – Lev. 11

Clean food for a cleansed people if they are to be healthy. The Christian is to be watchful – called upon to partake of that which speaks of cleanliness unto the Lord and to shun that which typified the unclean and love of this world.

Cloven footed, parteth the hoof, Psa. 1:1	Separated Walk, 2 Cor. 6:17
Cheweth the cud, Psa. 1:2	Meditation upon the Word
v. 4-8 Outwardly or partly alright but of the filth and earth – James 4:4; 1 Cor. 2:15; Phil. 1:9-10	Discernment
v. 9 Fins and scales not easily overturned – Eph. 4:14	Be Established. Fins – balance, driving force. Scales – protective coat.
Carrion (birds of prey), birds, insects to be shunned – v. 13-20, 1 Tim. 6:11	Forsake
Insects with wings – v. 21-22; Col. 3:2. Owl – flies at night. Cuckow – steals nests – devil – stealthy character.	Partake. Some insects – homes in filth.
Lev. 11:21 – could partake of grasshopper. They are stronger than humans for their size.	We must ascend spiritually.
Chameleon – always adjusts to environment	James 1:8

Leprosy – Lev. 13-14 – A type of sin

The lepers to live outside the camp – sin not only separates from God but puts a barrier between fellow man. Gen. 3:24; 4:16.

The Day of Atonement – Lev. 16

Two goats taken once a year to atone for sin of whole nation. One slain, the other having sins confessed on his head bore iniquity away into the wilderness. Lev. 16:21-22; John 1:29; Jer. 31:34; Heb. 10:4; Heb. 13:12-13; Isa. 43:25; Heb. 9:14.

The Value of the Blood Declared – Lev. 17:11-14

The value of the death of Christ is in the fact that He was the eternal Son of God who poured out His soul unto death.

It is from chapter 18 onwards that the phrase "I am the Lord" occurs so frequently as application is made to the personal conduct of the people. Jehovah is not only their redeemer, He is also the Lord of their life. Col. 1-3

Positionally they are made Holy by Sacrifice – Chap. 1-17	Eph. 1-3; Heb. 1-10; Col. 1-3
Practically they are called upon to be Holy in Conduct – Chap. 18-27	Eph. 4-6; Heb. 11-13; Col. 4

The Sanctity of Married Life – Lev. 18

Warning against grosser forms of Immorality – still has its application today in the moral realm, but also it may be applied in the spiritual realm.

The Conduct of Priests – Lev. 21-22

May be summarized as:

- What the Priest must do – Lev. 21:1-15

- What he must be – Lev. 21:16-24; 2 Pet. 1:4-9 (growth essential) : 1 John 2:9

- What he must offer – Lev. 22:17-33, noting especially v. 21. All the sons of Aaron were Priests by reason of birth and membership of Aaron's family – Lev. 21:22. Not all allowed to officiate or exercise the priestly office – Lev. 21:16-24. A blemish, etc. disqualified him 'that he profane not.' Notice the twelve references to "profane" in these two chapters. There was no provision for the miraculous removal of infirmities of the Priest, but for the believer there is the blood that cleanseth from all sin and the fire of God's Holy Spirit which purifies and fits for the Lord's service. The difference might be stated in the following two ways:

1. Our Standing, that is <u>Union</u> with Christ
2. Our State, that is <u>Communion</u> with Christ.

Blind man couldn't be a priest – we mustn't be spiritually blind. We are God's priests.

Lame – up and down in Christian life. Broken-handed – people can't depend on you – Eph. 4:17;

2 Tim. 4:10; 1 Cor. 5:11-13. Flat nose – must be able to sense the things that are unspiritual. Crooked back – must be upright in character. Dwarf – many Christians aren't useable because they are dwarfs. Lev. 21:16-24.

The Feasts of the Lord – Lev. 23

Times of fellowship. Passover – separation or salvation. Unleavened bread – sanctification.

It is noteworthy that in John's gospel 5:1 and 6:4 they are called 'Feasts of the Jews." Originally designed to keep God in the thought and to promote national and social life, especially the welfare of poor and servants. The better term would probably be 'set or special seasons' or 'holy days,' for they were times which God called the people to set aside and observe as times of rest for worship and thanksgiving. Seven such periods or seasons are mentioned here whereas only three, the Passover, Pentecost and Tabernacles were actually feasts in which all males were required to present themselves before the Lord.

A. The Sabbath of the Lord – A day of rest. Mark 2:27-28; Lev. 23:2-3. We must rest from our own works.

B. The Passover v. 4-14 also known as the Feast of Unleavened Bread. Mark 14:12; Acts 20:6. Commemorated deliverance from Egypt – observed seven days during which time only unleavened bread was to be eaten – leaven the symbol of moral corruption and sin

– abstention for seven days signified complete separation from evil. 1 Cor. 5:7-8 First and last of these seven days to be a Sabbath v. 6-7. Man at rest from his own work. During this feast, two or three sheaves of harvest v.22 waived before the Lord as a token or foretaste of coming harvest. It was the first fruit 1 Cor. 15:20, 23 Christ, the first fruit in heaven.

C. Pentecost – CONSECRATION – v. 20-22 – also known as the Feast of Weeks, of First Fruits or harvest. Observed 50 days after Passover, and kept for one day. Note the difference – the Passover barley sheaf marked commencement of grain harvest; i.e, sheaf direct from God's harvest.

The Pentecost wave loaves marked its completion – in the loaves the grain was ready for man's food.

Acts 2:1 2 Cor. 1:22; 5:5; Eph. 1:14 The Holy Spirit in the heart of the believer is the first fruits, the guarantee and the foretaste of coming glory – the harvest being an accomplished fact in the hearts of believers, it is by the Holy Spirit that Christ has become the living bread for the child of God. 23:17 'Baked with leaven' – true to type – even in blood-bought child of God who is indwelled by the Holy Spirit and joined to the life of Christ, sin yet remains. Hence, sin offering v. 19 denoting acceptance and communion through the sacrifice of Christ despite presence of evil in the nature.

D. Blowing of Trumpets – TESTIMONY – v. 23-25 – ushering in the civil year. Trumpets also sounded on the 1st of each month – dedication. There was a gap of 3 ½ months between Pentecost and Trumpets. Num. 10:1-10. 7th month. Ex. 14:13. Probably has reference to the regathering of Israel. Matt. 24:31; Zech. 9:14 but note also 1 Cor. 14:16; 15:52; 1 Thess. 4:16; 1 Cor. 14:7-8 – clarity necessary. Worship, progress, arming for conflict, joy and gladness, recognition of spiritual need.

E. Atonement – CONFESSIONS AND CLEANSING - v. 26-32 – the removal or covering of the sin of the nation. Tenth day of seventh month – it was to be a day of affliction and repentance. 1

John 2:2; 4:10. After entering into the Holy place, the High Priest shall come forth and put on his High Priestly robes – the coming forth has not yet been fulfilled. Heb. 9:24-28; Zech. 12:9-14.

F. Tabernacles – PILGRIMAGE AND PROVISION – v. 33-36 – also known as Feast of Booths or Ingathering. Held for seven days and kept five days after Atonement to remind of days of sojourning after deliverance from Egypt. 1 Pet. 2:11. A time of great joy. v. 40 also Zech. 14:16-20.

The Sabbth of Rest. Lev. 25:4, 10. Seven means perfection, completeness.

Every 7th year a Sabbatic year and every 50th year a Jubilee year. It was to be a rest – good for the land – for the people in developing faith in the Lord. v. 2-22 and preventive of covetousness, greed, accumulation of wealth – for servants – for cattle and beasts. The Jubilee year brought liberation to slaves, property and ground. Sabbath year – rest from toil, cancellation of debt. The Sabbatical year of Rest probably foreshadows the Millennial Reign of Christ upon earth so no doubt the year of Jubilee which brought liberty foreshadows the period of untold joy when there shall be no more curse – yet both have a fulfillment in the Christian life now. The life of Christ reigning in the heart gives wonderful rest and liberty now and a ceasing from our own work. Heb. 4:9-10. Levitical System is a circle of sevens – every 7th day a Sabbath – Every 7th year a Sabbatical year – every 7 times 7 years followed by year of Jubilee. Every 7th month is especially holy commencing with a Sabbath and having three feasts. Seven weeks between Passover and Pentecost – Passover observed seven days – Tabernacles observed seven days.

- At Passover – 14 lambs offered daily
- At Tabernacles – 14 lambs daily and 70 bullocks
- At Pentecost – 7 lambs
- Jubilee year – year of release of bond servants – Luke 4:19.

1 Cor. 14:33,40 Note the emphasis on order.

Obedience and Disobedience results in Blessing and Cursing - Lev. 26

Particulars contained in this chapter now largely history. Proof of God's foreknowledge – of divine inspiration of Scriptures – note 14 onwards and 44, 45. The Jew, the miracle of history now being regathered in readiness for Zech. 12:10-13:1.

The Special Vows - Lev. 27 - Non-obligatory

The overflow of love 2 Cor. 9:7

In Genesis	Abel's sacrifice	Covering for personal sin
Exodus	Passover sacrifice	Covering for the sin of the family
Leviticus	Atonement sacrifice	Covering for sin of the nation

Note: Atonement in O.T. – 'to cover' this was all the blood of beasts could do. John 1:29. It needed the blood of the Lamb of God <u>to remove</u> sin. Rom. 3:25.

NUMBERS

Read the whole book, especially noting chapters 13 and 14, chapter 22:1 to 25:6 and chapter 31:1-8. Also read 1 Cor. 10:1-14, especially noting verse 12, and Hebrews 3:1 to 4:16.

TITLE - The name of the Book comes from the Greek 'arithmoi' which in Latin becomes "numeri.' It is called Numbers because of the two numberings or census of the children of Israel, at Sinai (603,550) – chapter 1 and in Moab (601,730) – chapter 26. Hebrew name – B'mitbar – "in the wilderness." Over age 20 go to war. About 2 million people in all.

KEY WORDS - Warfare – Wandering – Journeying.

KEY VERSES - 14:6-9

HISTORIC PERIOD - approximately 40 years – Chapters 1-10, 20 days : Chapters 10-36, 39 years.

Chapters 15-19, 37-38 yrs. - Chapters 20-36, 1 year.

The Old Generation, born in Egypt

| Preparation for the Journey | Numbering of men of war – the arrangements and constitution of camp – consecration of Levites constituting the people into a nation and religious community. | 1:1 to 10:10 |

Advance – Rebellion and Rejection	Murmuring due to spies report	10:11 to 14:45
The Pilgrims become Wanderers	37 years interruption of the journey	15:1 to 19:22

The New Generation, born in wilderness

Preparation for Possession of the Land. Chapter 20:1 to 36:13. The continuation of the journey followed by victory.

CENTRAL CHAPTERS - 13 and 14: Chief Characters – Moses, Joshua and Caleb.

Chapters 22-24 Balaam's prophecy

The Message of the Book in relation to the Book of Leviticus:

LEVITICUS	NUMBERS
The call to worship	The call to walk with God
The call to Purity	The call to Pilgrimage
Spiritual position and relationship	Spiritual progress and responsibility
Fellowship with God	Faithfulness to God

The outstanding Message of the whole narrative may be summarized as follows:

- Beware of Unbelief. The People of God have the Promises of God that they might perform the Purpose of God. God had brought them out and had given the promise to bring them into the land – Ex. 6:6 and 8.

- God's people are called to Pilgrimage and Journeying, that is, to Progress – to be warriors, not wanderers. Chapters 15 to 19 cover nearly 38 years spent out of God's will – wasted ineffective years. Hebrews 5:11 to 6:1; 1 Corinthians 3:3.

- God is not the Author of Confusion – such time and space is taken to declare the orderly arrangement and service of the camp and tabernacle – Chapters 1 to 10; 1 Corinthians 14:33 and 40.

- The abiding Faithfulness of God. Through unbelief the people may wander and not enter into the blessing, but are not forsaken by God. He cannot deny Himself or His Word – 2 Tim. 2:13; Deut. 8:2-5; Lam. 3:22-23

- God cannot be Defeated – neither by the enemies of God nor by the failure of His own people. By human calculation it appears that man can postpone fulfillment but never can ultimate end be changed. 2 Pet. 3:12 – we can hasten His coming.

SPIRITUAL AND TYPICAL TEACHING

- Tracing of their Pedigree or Genealogy – Chapter 1. Of great importance if they were to prove their claim to and inheritance in the land and fight the battles of the Lord. None of the mixed multitude allowed to fight – 1:45 – the Lord's people for the Lord's work. Be sure of our spiritual standing – John 3:3 and 6; Romans 8:16; Rom. 9; 1 Pet. 3:15; Matt. 7:22-23.

- The Privilege and Responsibility of Serving the Lord by Giving – Chap. 7. Each ruler gave exactly the same – each noted separately. Mark 12:41-45; 2 Cor. 9:7; 1 Cor. 16:1-2; Acts 20:35.

- The Lighting of the Candlestick. Chap. 8:2-4. To shed light abroad and reveal the beauty of the candlestick of beaten gold. The oil gave light through the branches. The Holy Spirit living in and flowing through the Church and individuals enables believers to be lights unto the world, and should reveal the beauty of the Lord Jesus. John 8:12; 9:5; Matt. 5:14-16; Rev. 1:12-13, 20.

- Cleansing and Setting apart of Levites – Chap. 8. The males of the tribe of Levi were set apart in place of the first born of the other tribes – 3:40. Their cleansing was twofold: (1) Sprinkles upon, 8:7 God's work. (2) Shaved all flesh and washed their clothes, 7 – man's responsibility. The child of God is cleansed but required to purity himself, shaving off even things which seem as much a part of us as our hair. Rom. 12:1-2; 2 Cor. 6:14 to 7:1. The Levites were accepted on the grounds of sacrifice, v. 8 and 12 and were wholly offered unto the Lord, v. 13 to 16; 1 John 3:3; Rev. 1:5-6; 5:10.

- The Pillar of Cloud by Day and Pillar of Fire by Night. Chap. 9:15-23; 10:11-13 & 34; 12:5. Symbolic of the Lord's presence, every movement of the camp regulated by God. A picture of the Lord's unfailing guidance – Prov. 3:5-6; Psa. 25:5-6 (meek/teachable); 25:9 and 12; 32:8; Isa. 30:21; John 8:12.

- Six silver trumpets - Chap. 10:1-10 – called the people to worship, war, service or advance. Note the instructions in verses 3-5, etc.; Psa. 12:6; John 10:27. Privilege of the sons of Aaron to sound the trumpets v. 8. 1 Cor. 14:8-12; Num. 10:29 (Hobab knew the area – led with Moses).

- The Outcome of the Complaining and Murmuring – Chap. 11.

  (a) Dissatisfaction with God's provision – after only three days v. 1 – by the mixed multitude, verses 4-6.

  (b) Requests granted, but... verses 4 and 20; Psalm 78:29; Psa. 106:14-15

  (c) Jealousy and Pride, effecting even the High Priest, Aaron and prophetess, Miriam – Chap. 12. Note verses 3 and 13 and God's vindication of His servant, v. 5-8.

  (d) Unbelief – this kept the people out of the land of blessing. Ten spies saw the difficulty – two saw God first and the difficulties in their proper perspective. Human unbelief cannot prevent the purposes of God but appear to postpone their fulfillment.

  Unbelief robs. Belief inherits. Personal loss or personal reward.

- The Good Report of the Land – Chap. 13:23-27. Even those who are not prepared to enter in agree upon the good of the Christian experience. The Sermon on the Mount and Gal. 5:22-23. The People had now ceased to be Pilgrims and become Wanderers.

- God's Dealing with His people in the Wilderness - Chap. 15:1; Deut. 8:2-6; 29:5-6.

  (a) Revealing His love and care – but note Chap. 15:30-36 – to disobey is to reproach the Lord. The willful scorning of God, for which God will not hold man guiltless.

  (b) Reminder that they are His people – the [tassel] of blue Chap. 15:38-41, heavenly color to remind them of God's Word and that they are His people.

- Aaron's Rod which Budded – Chap. 17. A picture of the resurrection of Christ – preceded by Chap. 17:3 – that which was dead made to live and the rod "brought forth almonds" v. 8. God thus testifying to His acceptance of the man of His choice and therefore of his sacrifice and high priestly office. v. 5; Acts 3:14-16 and 4:10; Phil. 2:8-9; Heb. 2:9-10; Rom. 1:3-4 Christ's holiness and His resurrection indicate His sovereignty (son of God).

- The water of Separation – Chap. 19. Cleansing from Defilement in daily life. The ashes of a red heifer which had been offered and wholly consumed without the camp mingled with running water. v. 17 speaks of continual cleansing based on atonement. 1 John 1:7; John 3:5,10,12; John 13:1-11.

- Moses' Unbelief – Chap. 20:7-11. Compare v. 8 and 11. Spiritual maturity never places us beyond the possibility of a fall. Gal. 6:1-3; 1 Cor. 10:12. Nevertheless God graciously allowed the water to flow. Moses acted hastily – smote rock twice – broke picture of Christ on the cross.

- The Death of Miriam – Chap. 20:1 …of Aaron Chap. 20:23-29 (33:38-39) and sin of Moses. All emphasize that neither

Prophet – Priest – nor Lawgiver – can lead into the Promised Land. Fullness of blessing can only be experienced under the leadership of Joshua. The people again become Pilgrims and Warriors. It took 48 hours to bring them out of Egypt but 40 years to take Egypt out of them!

- A New Beginning marked by Answers to Prayer – Chap. 21:3. Compare 14:45 and Deut. 1:34. Out of line to God's will suspends in some measure the power of prayer. Being in the will of God is to know the secret of answered prayer and victory over spiritual foes.

- The Serpent of Brass – Chap. 21. This is a very clear type of the saving power of the death of the Lord Jesus Christ.

- Then Israel Sang! Chap. 21:17. When did they last sing? The song of Moses Ex. 15:1; Col. 3:15-16

- Balaam's Prophecy – Chap. 22-24. Also 31:8 and 16. Balaam comes from Padan-Aram. Chap. 22:5 and Deut. 23:4; Num. 23:7. Abraham and Laban once dwelt. Gen. 28:5. Balaam is a strange, paradoxical character. Compare 22 v. 12, 18, 19, 20, 34. The whole incident illustrated the Sovereignty of God – it is impossible to fight against God. Acts 5:39. One has no right to pray about things stated definitely against God's will in His Word.

- Did Balaam's ass speak? Chap. 22:22-35, again noting verses 34 and 35; 2 Pet. 2:15. Note the following prophetic utterances: Chap. 23:9-10; 24:5-9, 15-19 and Matt. 2:2; Rev. 22:16. Balaam's End – Chap. 31:8. Three-fold reference in the New Testament – Rev. 2:14; 2 Pet. 2:15; Jude 11.

Following points are worthy of special notice.

(a) The request of the daughters of Zelophehad – Chap. 27:1-7.

(b) The request of Moses – Chap. 27:12-17

(c) The Charging of Joshua – Chap. 27:18-23

(d) The Victory over the Midianites without loss – Chap. 31:49. What further victories there might have been in Canaan!

(e) The Request of Reuben, Gad and the half tribe of Manasseh – Chap. 32:1. "when they saw." Failure to go the whole way with God – result 1 Chron. 5:18-26.

(f) The six Cities of Refuge – Chap. 35:6; Heb. 6:18.

CHAPTER	FAILED
11	Nation
12	Miriam and Aaron
13	10 spies
14	Nation
16-17	Korah, Dathan and Abiram
20	Moses

DEUTERONOMY

Read the whole book particularly noting chapters 27-30; 31:30 – 32:47.

TITLE - The Name comes from the Greek and means "The Second Law." The new generation had grown up and the previous generation who heard the Law when first given at Mount Sinai forty years before, had passed away. Therefore, the new generation has the Law Rehearsed and emphasized to them.

Hebrew Name – "Words" or "These are the words."

KEY WORDS - Obedience, Remember (past) and Obey (in the future)

KEY VERSES - 5:29; 10:12-13; 11:26-28; 28:1-2, 13

HISTORIC PERIOD - The book contains eight discourses delivered on the Plains of Moab, one month before entering the Promised Land. 1:1-3.

SHORT SUMMARIES OF CONTENTS -

I. Retrospect 1-11 Remember – Reflect

II. Prospect 12-34 Anticipation 'Keep' – 'Obey' – 'do'

I. Historical 1 – 4:49

II. Legislative 5 – 26:19

III. Prophetic 27-32:47

IV. Conclusion – the final words of God to Moses, the blessing of the Tribes and the death of Moses

32:48 – 34:12

A more complete Summary is as follows:

Review of Israel's wandering and God's long suffering	1:1 – 4:43	The past reviewed
The First Discourse	1:5-4:40	
Three Cities of Refuge	4:41-43	
Repetition and Exposition of the Law	4:44-26	The law restated
The Second Discourse, covering Moral, Civil and Ceremonial Law		
God's Future Purposes	27-30	The future revealed
The Third Discourse – the distant future	27-28	
The Fourth Discourse – the immediate future	29-30	
Record of Closing Events of Moses' Life	31-34	The lawgiver's reward and removal
The Fifth Discourse	31:1-13	
Charge to Moses	31:14-24	
The Sixth Discourse	31:25-29	
The Seventh Discourse – Jehovah's command to Moses	31:30-32:47	
The Eighth Discourse	32:48-52	
Death and Burial of Moses – Death with a Vision	33:1-29	

THE BEST OF CAPERNWRAY

OUTSTANDING CHAPTERS - 27-30, 32, 33

OUTSTANDING CHARACTERISTICS -

- The Farewell Discourses of Moses – contain some of the world's finest eloquence. Compare Ex. 4:10
- Two Major Prophecies

A. The coming Messiah 18:15-19; John 5:46; Acts 3:22; 7:37

B. Israel's future – particularly 28:49-57. The terrible details are both fulfilled in the Roman and Babylonian sieges of Jerusalem. John 1:21-25; 5:46; 6:14.

The Importance of Deuteronomy

It refers back to the previous four books of Moses 259 times.

30 references to Genesis

94 " to Exodus

61 " to Leviticus

74 " to Numbers

Find similarities between Moses and the Lord – deliverer – law-giver – mediator

Deuteronomy is quoted or referred to 356 times in the later books of the Old Testament. Deut. – a key stone.

In the New Testament, it is said to be quoted or referred to 96 times in 17 of the 27 books.

Our Lord's three replies to the devil in the wilderness were taken from Deuteronomy 6:13, 16; 8:3; Matt. 4:4, 7, 10.

Our Lord also quoted Deut. 6:5 as the greatest commandment. Matt. 22:37-38; Mark 12:29-30.

The use of it by the Lord no doubt accounts for the particularly fierce attacks made upon the book by the higher critics (attack Gen., Deut., and Daniel); we suggest that the writing is of a later date and indeed 'a pious fraud' written within the reign of Josiah. 2 Kings 23. This is not proved on textural grounds but particular reference to a central place of worship was made in view of the immediately impending entry and possession of the Promised Land. Both Stephen and Peter clearly quoted the book as the words of Moses. Quoting from Deut. 18 – Acts 7:37; 3:22. Our Lord would never have quoted the words of a 'pious fraud' to silence the adversary – nor would Satan have been silenced by anything other than the authoritative Word of God.

Reviews the past with an eye to the future.

THE MESSAGE OF THE BOOK

The first four books of Moses lead naturally from one to the other. Deuteronomy embraces them all as it reviews the past with an eye to the future.

- The Love of God is the Ground of God's dealings with His People. This book declares the love and goodness of God as the ground of God's governmental grace. 6:24; 10:12-13.

- God's love to man Calls for Man's love to God. This is to be the motive for obedience. 10:12-13; 11:1, 13, 22; 19:9. It is worthy to note the emphasis on love as the fulfilling of the law. Rom. 13:10 in view of Jewish boast in performance which excluded love. Matt. 25:23. The above two points combine John's great declaration 1 John 4:19.

- The Deliverance was with a view to inheritance 6:23. They were not only saved from bondage in Egypt – they were to enter into a life of fullness of blessing in the Promised Land. The believer is saved not only to be saved but to enter into all that God has made available in Christ. John 10:10; Gal. 2:20; Eph. 1:3-4; 3:16-19; 5:18; 1 Thess. 5:23.

- To witness to and Teach the Unity of God – 6:4. In Israel's day heathen worshipped a multiplicity of gods. Israel's great witness to the one true God.

SPIRITUAL AND TYPICAL TEACHING

1. The Prophet who was to come. 18:13. Note the points of likeness between Moses and the Lord Jesus.

2. The Cities of Refuge – 4:41; 19:1 in which man-slayers might find safety and peace and deliverance from their adversaries.

3. The Curse pronounced upon those who were Hung upon a Tree. 21:22-23; Gal. 3:13.

4. The Urim and Thummim 33:8. The two Hebrew words mean light and perfection. John 8:12 : Col. 2:3.

5. The Life of Moses – the man of God – 34:10 deserves special study, specially noting the three divisions of 40 years. Acts 7:18-44.

Note Deuteronomy 33:27.

Moses's Farewell Message may be summed up in three phrases: Know God Love God Obey God

Deut. 6:3-9 Know the Word. John 15:7 – "if ye abide in me, and my words abide in you ye shall ask what ye will and it shall be done unto you."

JOSHUA

Read the whole Book and also the Epistle to the Ephesians.

Title and Authorship. Joshua means 'Jehovah saves.' In Greek New Testament it is Jesus – 'Savior.' Acts 7:45; Heb. 4:8.

The traditional view is that Joshua either actually wrote or supplied the material. The Talmud asserts Joshua wrote all except the last five verses which may have been added by Phinehas – 24:33.

From chapter 15:63 it must have been written before the time of David. From 6:25 it must have been written while Rahab was still alive. The expression "to this day" occurs bout 14 times, signifying that the writing was contemporary with the events recorded.

The Book itself makes no claim to be the work of a certain author.

KEY WORDS – Possession or Possess your Possessions

KEY VERSES – 1:2-3; 21:44-45; 11:23

HISTORIC PERIOD – Approximately 1451 to 1426 B.C. – about 25 years.

1050 years from Joshua's time to end of O.T. time

Comparison of Moses and Joshua – together they form a type of Christ – Deuteronomy 6:23.

Moses means 'drawn out' – Joshua – 'Salvation of Jehovah' or 'Savior'

Great event in Moses's life – crossing the Red Sea.

THE BEST OF CAPERNWRAY

In Joshua's life – crossing Jordan.

The Red Sea emphasizes deliverance through Christ's death. Redemption.

Jordan emphasizes the new life made available by His resurrection.

Gal. 2:20; Rom. 6:1-11 (especially v. 4-6); Col. 2:12

Moses's symbol – the rod – speaking of Good Shepherd. John 10:1-28.

Joshua's symbol – the spear – the Lord shall fight for you. Rom. 13:14; 1 Tim. 6:12

SUMMARY OF CONTENTS

Entrance	The Land Entered. Charge to Joshua. Faith of Rahab. The Memorial Stones.	1:1 – 5:12
Conquest	The Land Conquered. Fall of Jericho. Defeat at and conquest of Ai. Further Conquests.	5:13 – 12:24
Possession	The Land Possessed. Allocation to various tribes, including Cities of Refuge and Cities for the Levites.	13 - 22
Continuance	The Warrior's Farewell Charge to his people. "Be ye very courageous" "be ye doers of the Word" "Cleave unto the Lord"	23-24

Note:

1. The Christophany – Joshua 5:13-15.

2. Joshua's Plan of Campaign – first of all to drive a wedge into the Center of the land – Thothmes - ch. 6-9. Then he turned to the Conquest of the South – ch. 10, and finally to the Conquest of the North – ch. 11.

HISTORIC ACCURACY

The Book has been assailed for several reasons; chiefly on account of its miracles.

1. The Invasion of Palestine. Joshua is referred to in the Tel-el-Amarna Tablets in a message to Pharaoh. These same Tablets also record the invasion of Palestine by the Habiru and contain appeals to Pharaoh for help. One such appeal came from the King of Uruslim and reads "The Habiru are occupying the King's cities. There remains not one prince to my lord, the King; everyone is ruined." Professor Garstang identified the Habiru with the Hebrews. How did God prepare the way for His people? Joshua 24:12. Power of the Hittite Empire and that of the Amorites was broken by Thothmes the third, brother of Pharaoh's daughter – Ex. 2. The hornet was the personal emblem of Thothmes the third and part of the Egyptian national emblem. Israel had become weakened.

2. Crossing of Jordan – Ch. 3. The Creator is able to intervene and controls natural laws – no difficulty if you know in your heart the greater miracle of the new birth.

3. The Fall of Jericho – Professor Garstang has proved from Archaeological discovery that the walls actually fell flat; in reality there were two walls across which houses were built – also proved the city was not packed but utterly destroyed by fire when it was not forsaken but full of life. Professor Garstang in his book *Joshua and Judges* writes "Joshua, in fulfilling God's command, little thought he was providing the very evidence which would vindicate the truth of God's Word to sceptics and unbelievers 3,000 years later." Jericho like a fort – nomads would flee in times of danger to the city. About 6 miles from Jordan.

4. The Long Day – ch. 10. Astronomically calculated and proved correct by Professor Totten of U.S.A. and E.W. Maunder of Greenwich Royal Observatory. Professor Totten calculates it to 23 hrs. 20 min. In chapter 10:13 it is referred to as being

recorded historically in Jasher's account. In Greek, Egyptian, Chinese and Indian ancient records there are all references to an abnormally long day. Heroditus (Gr. Historian) – 480 B.C. states that Egyptian Priests told him of a day such as this. The Hindu records state the event happened in the year Cali 1651 which corresponds exactly with 1451 B.C. 2 Kings 20:11.

5. The Extermination of the Canaanites – Deut. 20:16-18. Compare Gen. 15:16 and 2 Peter 3:9. Leviticus 18 reveals the immorality of the Canaanites and this has similarly been proved by the images and revolting idols which have been excavated. Canaanites given to Spiritism or spiritualism. Deut. 18:10-14.

6. The Reading of the Law on Mt. Ebal and Mt. Gerizim – 8:30-35. Ebal means "heap of stones," the Mt. of Cursing. Gerizim – "cutting down," The Mount of Blessing or Olive Yards. The acoustic properties of this valley have been tested – it has been proved possible for the human voice to be heard from summit to summit, although they are 1 ½ miles apart.

7. The Destruction by Fire of Ai – ch. 8; ch. 10:32; Debir – 10:39; Hazor – 11:10-11 have all been proved accurate by archaeological expeditions; namely, Kyle Memorial Expedition 1934, and the Welcome Expedition 1931.

The Message of the Book. As John's Gospel is related to the previous three gospel narratives, so Deuteronomy stands in relation to the previous four books of Moses, and Joshua stands in the same relation to the books of Moses and Acts does to the Gospels.

The Epistle to the Ephesians also has a correspondence with the Book of Joshua.

In Deuteronomy	In Joshua
Sets forth future prospect	Prospect becomes present experience
Reveals the vision of faith	Faith is called upon to venture
Victory is promised	Victory is achieved
The book of Possibilities	The book of realization

Note how these points sum up in some measure the relationship of Acts to the Gospels.

The Outstanding Message of the whole Book may be summarized as follows:

1. "Great is Thy Faithfulness" – Lam. 3:23. God is able to perform that which He promises. 1:2-5.

2. Men must Accept to Enjoy. The great spiritual principle is revealed that that which God gives must always be accepted to be enjoyed – applies to salvation and all Christian experience. Faith is seen acting, taking the receiving the fulfillment of the promises. 1:3.

3. <u>God only stops giving when ceases to continue to take</u> – 18:3; 1 Thess. 5:19. Exercise of faith and total obedience essential.

4. To Ensure the Continuance of Victory, there can never be Compromise.

5. God is ever at war with Sin. God never lowers His standard. Jesus Christ the same yesterday, today and forever. Heb. 13:8.

6. Joshua rose early in the morning - 3:1; 6:12, 15; 7:16; 8:10,14.

Comparison between Ephesians and Joshua

In the Epistle to the Ephesians there is a five-fold reference to the phrase "in the heavenlies" which speaks of the vital union of the believer with the life of the risen Christ. Spiritually, the inheritance in the promised land speaks of this.

	Ephesians
The promised inheritance is predestined for a chosen people	1:3-5
The inheritance is made available by the entrance in of God's chosen Man	1:18-22
The inheritance is entered by grace through faith and is God's gift	2:5-8

The possession of the inheritance is to make known and declare the wisdom and glory of God	3:6-11
The inheritance is also the place of conflict with powerful enemies – provision has been made for complete victory by reason of Eph. 1:20-21; 6:10-11 and 13-18	6:12

THE TYPICAL AND SPIRITUAL TEACHING

The Promised Land is typical of the life of fullness in Christ – it speaks of the victorious life. For Israel it was a land, for the believer it is a life of infinite resources because it is not Canaan but Christ.

Ch. 1 Governing principles set out for entering into Canaan:

Readiness to act in faith	1:1
Count upon the Lord's presence and promise – 'the land I have given you'	1:3,5,9
We must 'be strong & of a good courage.' Unbelief & doubt always lead to failure & fear	1:6,7,9
Obey the Word of the Lord. To obey it you must know it. 'Abiding' - obeying	1:7,8

Four general characteristics of the land:

- Rest from wandering – Deut. 6:10-11; Matt. 11:28-29; Heb. 4:3
- Living Water – Deut. 8:7; John 4:14; 7:37-38
- Plenty – Deut. 8:8-9; Eph. 1:3. Fertility, wealth (mineral), fruitfulness – Gal. 5:22-23; John 12:11; Phil 4:13, 19; 1 Cor. 1:30
- Promise of victory – Deut. 11:25; Rom. 8:37. They were forewarned their enemies were greater but they were conquerors – 1 Cor. 15:57; 1 John 5:4,5

The Difference between Inheritance and Possession:

Inheritance is that which God gives to His people. Possession is that which His people choose to take and make their own.

Rehab – ch. 2 demonstrates the way of Salvation. Heb. 11:31. Among other points, note Rahab's token is called by three names – cord, Scarlet thread, Line.

'Cord' v. 15 made up of several strands denoting strength – Eccl. 4:12. The strength of our salvation is the three-fold work of God the Father, God the Son and God the Holy Spirit.

'Scarlet thread' v. 18 emphasizes its distinctive nature – 1 Pet. 1:18-19

'Line' v. 18:21 The word used for line is used elsewhere in O.T., 2 times referred to for hope. 1 Pet. 1:3. Note Rehab in Matt. 1:5 and James 2:25. Rahab hears, acts and is willing to obey.

The Crossing of Jordan – ch. 4.

The fulfillment of the Red Sea crossing – Psa. 114:3,5; Heb. 11:29-30. For the believer, one event, but often two in experience. Rom. 6:1-11. The Memorial Stones witness to being buried and risen with Christ. Col. 3:2-3; Gal. 2:20. Believer's identification with the death of Christ.

In ch. 5 the crossing of Jordan is followed by "circumcision," "Passover," "feeding on old corn of the land."

Our entrance into the fullness of the life in Christ is essentially that which God does, Resurrection (coming through Jordan) but it must also be accompanied by Renunciation (circumcision) which is man's part. 1 John 3:1,2

Restoration of fellowship and identification with Christ in His death (Passover) is followed by feeding, dependence upon the risen life of Christ (the old corn on the land). Then we are prepared for the Revelation of 5:13-14, that Christ comes not to help, but to Captain and Command us. Unbelief causes us to hesitate. When we act we know God is as good as His Word; Word is true.

The Christian life is a warfare – ch. 5:13-15; 5:11-12 – began to eat of the fruit of the land. Emphasized throughout narrative. It has its counterpart in Eph. 6:10-18; Isa. 9:6; Matt. 28:18.

THE BEST OF CAPERNWRAY

Israel's enemies were three-fold:

Egyptians	The World
Amalekites	The Flesh, self-life
In Canaan, The Canaanites	Canaanites, by reason of their corruption, appear to be a type of the very devil himself

The Fall of Jericho – ch. 6; 2 Cor. 10:3-4. GOD'S WAY of victory, He accomplished it. Obedience to God is greater wisdom. Why walk around? Tires you out before fighting. God's way.

The Key phrases of ch. 6 are significant:

	Sign of	Referred to	
The ark of the covenant	God's Presence	10 times	1 Cor. 15:58; Rom. 8:37; 1 John 2:14; 5:3-5
The Trumpet or Ram's Horns	G-d's Power	14 times	
The Priests – it was their duty to see that the Law was observed & there were therefore the keepers	The People's Purity	9 times	John 17:15-19 - sanctification

Defeat at Ai – ch. 7 – MAN'S WAY

Through sin of Achan. Compare 7:21 with Gen. 3:6,8. Contemplation of sin invariably leads to sinful actions. James 1:13-15; 1 John 2:15-17. Unconfessed and unforsaken sins bring defeat – 1 John 1:9, whereas fellowship restored brings victory – 8:1. Valuable to note that even <u>the promises of God give no ground for self-confidence</u> – 7:3.

The Ruse of the Gibeonites – ch. 9 – ADVERSARY'S WAY

Teach the subtlety of the adversary's tactics – 2 Cor. 2:11; 1 Pet. 5:8; 2 Cor. 11:4 1 Cor. 2:15; Heb. 5:14 – ability to distinguish between that which is or isn't of God. The Safeguard – James 1:15; Psa. 25:9 in contrast to Joshua 9:14.

Caleb – the Example and Reward of Faith – 14:6-15.

For him, years had not dimmed the promises of God. Note Num. 14:24. Six times in O.T. is expression "wholly following the Lord" used and five times it is of Caleb whose name means "whole-hearted" – Phil. 3:13-14 – "apprehend" – laid hold of. The end of the race is the most important!

Three Different Attitudes adopted by the Tribes.

How do they compare to our attitude in facing Christian life: 17:16 'not enough'; 19:9 'too much'; 19:47 'too little.'

The Cities of Refuge – ch. 20

Six cities of refuge for murders by intent or accidental murders. Free after death of high priest or until they had a fair trial. Six – imperfect number – Heb. 6:18.

Ex. 21:13; Num. 35; Deut. 4:41-43; 19:1-13. The Seventh City – Heb. 6:18

The Altar of Witness – ch. 22

Misunderstanding of motives and actions. Desire for outer sign of unity – present today too. Recognize true unity already present. Eph. 4:3 'Endeavoring to keep the unity of the Spirit in the bond of peace.'

How easily misunderstandings arise! The desire for outward sign of unity; was it necessary?

Joshua – A Type of Christ leading into victory and possession. Contrast 24:29 with Heb. 7:16. Type of Christian believer – his call and command is by Word of God – 1:2-5, 9.

Called to be a type of Christ/disciple:

Soldier	Fighting – be strong	Ex. 17:9-16
Disciple	Learning	Ex. 17:14; 24:13-14; 32:17
Worshipper	Worshipping	Ex. 33:11
Witness	Testifying and Standing fast	Num. 14:6-10
Leader	Entering in – made a blessing	Deut. 1:38; 3:28; 31:7-8 ,22,23
Victor	Victorious	24:1-13.

The secret of Joshua's life and victory is in chapter 24 where the emphasis is "I," referring to Jehovah 17 times in verses 1-3. The believer's secret, Gal. 2:20

Hence, the significance of the renaming of Joshua by Moses – Joshua was originally Oshea, meaning 'Salvation.' This was changed to Je'hoshea, meaning 'Salvation of Jehovah,' and so to Joshua.

Israel was a theocracy ruled by God; a Monarchy – what they chose to be; Dependency – alien kings.

Theocracy – what God intended.

History – designed to teach us the ways of God. To reveal developments of Israel which was to trace the line of David. The Hebrews wrote history 1000 years before the great Greek historian, Heroditus.

Canaan – what we can enjoy now; not heaven.

JUDGES

Read the whole of the book, also Joshua 23:11-16 – forewarning. Jer. 2:7 and 17:9; 2 Cor. 6:17-18

TITLE - Hebrew name "Shophetim" meaning Judgment. The Judges is derived from special form of rulership which characterized this period of Israel's history. The Judges were really 'deliverers' or 'saviors,' but also were men raised up to bring the people into line with God's law – Ex. 18:16

DATE AND AUTHORSHIP - Rabbinic tradition ascribes the Book to Samuel. The evidence is certainly in favor of contemporary authorship. The geographic and other details such as reference to iron chariots have been verified by Professor Garstang. From chapter 17:6; 18:1; 19:1; 21:25 it is suggested that it was not written *prior to the event of 2 Sam. 5. At least twelve times there is a reference to Ephraim, which suggests that the writing was compiled from records kept at Shiloh and made very probably by Samuel or one of this disciples. The style certainly suggests one person as author.

KEY WORDS – Declension: Apostasy leading to Anarchy. Rebellion : Retribution : Repentance : Restoration (occurs 7 times)

KEY VERSES - 2:11-19; 17:6; 21:25 (every man did that which was right in his own eyes).

HISTORIC PERIOD – Chronologists vary in their computation of the period and put the date between 1426 and 1049 B.C. In referring to Jephthah who lived near the end of the period in 1126, 300 years is mentioned and Paul in Acts 13:20 says about 450 years. There are frequent references in the book to 40 years, but this may have been a round figure similar to our expression "generation." Judges 11:26 mentions 300-year period.

OUTSTANDING CHARACTERISTICS

- Contains the first parable in the Bible. Probably the oldest recorded parable – 9:8-15

- Deborah in chapter 4 is the first reference to a woman taking leadership in Israel's national life.

OUTSTANDING CHARACTERS

The fourteen Judges – most noteworthy being Deborah, Gideon, Jephthah and Samson. Ehud – 40 years a judge; others 20 years. O.T. "generation" – 40 years – period of testing frequently ending in trial.

OUTSTANDING CHAPTER

Chapter 5 – the Song of Deborah

SUMMARY OF CONTENTS

It is necessary to note that the contents are not always chronological, but there is purpose in the arrangement. The last five chapters, 17-21 belong to the earlier period of the book – see chapter 20:28 and 18:30 (to an apostate priest). Similarly chapter 1:1 – 2:5 is an overall summary of the period immediately following the death of Joshua. The Book reopens with specific details from chapter 2:5 to the end of chapter 18.

Introductory Summary	1:1 – 2:5
Main Contents	2:6 – 16:31
Appendix	17:1 – 21:25

*earlier than the time of Saul, while 1:21 implies it was written prior to the event of 1 Sam. 6.

FULLER SUMMARY

Partial Obedience – leading to declension and apostasy – chapter 1:1 to 3:6

Looks back to past failure – 1:1 – 2:10

Anticipates future failure – 2:11 – 3:6

History of Sevenfold Apostasy and Seven Deliverances – chapter 3:7 to 16:31

		Enemy		Peace
First	3:7-11	Mesopotamia	8 yrs subjection - deliverer Othniel	40 years
Second	3:12-31	Moabites, Amorites and Amalekites	18 years - Ehud	80 years
Third	4:1-5, 31	Canaanites	20 yrs - Deborah & Barak	40 years
Fourth	6:1-8, 32	Midianites	7 yrs - Gideon	40 years
Fifth	8:33-10, 5	Ursurpation of Abimelech	3 yrs - judgeship of Tola & Jair	45 years
Sixth	10:6-12, 15	Ammonites	18 yrs - Jephthah	31 years
Seventh	13:1-16	Philistines	40 yrs - Samson	20 years

People enjoyed more peace but subjection is stressed more – as a warning.

Appendix – revealing Anarchy arising from Apostasy – chapter 17:1 to 21:25

• Infidelity in Family Life	17-18
• Immorality in Home and Social Life	19
• Confusion in National Life, Prov. 14:34	20-21

Christophanies – the Angel of the Lord – Judges 2:1-5; 6:11; 13:3-21.

Pre-incarnation experiences of Christ

THE MESSAGE OF THE BOOK – a contrast to Joshua.

Joshua speaks of Progress and Possession and Spiritual Victory.

Judges speaks of Decline, Bondage and fleshly Defeat.

From the Book of Judges we are taught not to be presumptuous nor need we ever despair – Rom. 5:20b. Where sin abounds, grace doth much more abound.

1. The Faith and Supply of the Spirit for Yesterday will not meet the need of Today. You can never live on a past spiritual experience – 1 Cor. 9:26-27; Phil 3:13-14.

2. Partial Obedience and Compromise leads to Partial Victory and later Defeat. God said Judah shall go. Judah said Simeon help me. Note the tolerance of evil and first steps of apostasy – chapter 1:2-3 and 1:19 – only partial victory. 1:21 – written prior to when David drove them out. 1:27; 1:28 (they weren't to have Canaanites as servants). 1:21, 27-35; 6:7-10. Compare Deut. 7:1-3. Contrast 1 John 2:14 and Gal. 5:7. Only partial obedience such scriptures as Rom. 12:1-2; Eph. 4:1 and 5:17-18, etc., lays foundation for a life out of fellowship with God and of defeat.

3. Reveals God's Governmental Grace – God never abandons His people or His purpose but equally He never tolerates sin in His people. He bestows many privileges but never gives His people the privilege of sinning! God's Governmental grace is revealed in the sevenfold story of sin, punishment and deliverance – while sin produces chastisement, it is ever with the purpose to lead back to God and so to restoration – Heb. 12:5-11.

Note that which God has joined together:

Sin and Sorrow	Isa. 50:11; Psa. 16, 4
Repentance and Salvation	Judges 3:9; 3:15; 4:3-6; 6:6-8:11-12; 10:10, 15; 11:29; 13:5; Rom. 10

The truth of Jer. 17:9 is proved, Judges is a commentary on the incorrigible evil and wickedness of the human heart. Note how quickly they forgot the divine mercy and deliverance. 1 Cor. 15:10a.

THE TYPICAL AND SPIRITUAL TEACHING

The whole narrative is Typical of the Experience of the backsliding Christian – during this period the history of Israel was an 'up and down' experience.

1. Achsah's request – 1:12-15. Requested water – source of blessing. Be more concerned with the source of blessing than with outflow – the Blesser is more important than the blessing.

2. The Three-fold Reason given for Allowing the Enemy to Remain in the Land has valuable application.

   - to punish the people for disobedience – 2
   - to prove Israel's fidelity – 2:22-23
   - to teach those who knew nothing of warfare how to wage war – 3:1-2

   "Out of their weakness were made strong" – Heb. 11:34

   Summed up – the enemy in the land was to teach them the true nature of their heart and the source of their power. The presence of the old nature of sin and temptation reveals this to the child of God. Matt. 9:29; 2 Cor. 5:7; Gal. 5:16-17, 24-25. In conflict we also learn how to wage spiritual warfare – 2 Cor. 10:3-5.

3. Those Sent by God to be Deliverers were faint foreshadowings of the coming Savior – Heb. 11:32. God raised up the Deliverers from different tribes – born in obscure places and ordinarily of no consequence. 1 Cor. 1:26

4. Gideon illustrated the Transforming Power of God's Presence – 6:11 – 7:25; 8:35. Here is a man at first despondent, then conscious of his own inability but later conscious of the power and ability of God to meet the situation. Realization of his own weakness seen in demanding proof after proof from God but also so sure of God that he went against the powerful enemy

host with only 300 men, lamps, pitchers and trumpets. Deut. 20:8; Mark 8:7; 1 Cor. 1:26. Think over the following points:

Trinity of evil	6:3
The reason for bondage and servitude	6:10
Gideon's despondency and fearfulness	6:13-17
Gideon's gathering, threshing and hiding the grain?	6:11
Job 23:12; Psa. 119:9, 11, 16; Psa. 37:31	
The secret of strength and assurance – Matt. 1:23	6:12,14,16
God seeks a sign from Gideon	6:17
He did it by night	6:27
Further signs and testings	6:36-40
Details of triumphs. The greatness of 8:23 followed by the tragedy 8:24-27; Gal. 6:1; 1 Cor. 10:12-13	7:16-21

The Nazarite Order 13:5-7, 16-17; Num. 6:1-21; Amos 2:11 – Speaks of separation from the world is the will of God.

- Samson – the man of Uncompleted Service – Chap. 13-16. Samson's history is a sad story but so true to life. Born according to promise – called by God – equipped and used – but allowing his natural passions to reassert themselves. Yet we need to note that he is also the Man Who God Used Again – 16:28-30.

- Meditate on Jephthah's Great Declaration – 11:35.

Samson promised against human possibility. 13:5. Believers "born according to promise, for a purpose." 2 Pet 1:1-4; John 6:37,39; 1 John 2:25; Eph. 1:4; 2:10; 2 Thess. 2:13, 6; John 1:12

Samson born to be separated 13:5 & 7 – three marks of a Nazarite:

- Separate from things (wine or any product of the vine). Feed not on the dead things of the world

- Not to be contaminated by a dead person. If a person dropped dead at his side, his vow was broken. Couldn't attend funeral of family member. We are to be separate from the dead people of this life.

- Outward – long hair – couldn't be cut. Separation should be known. (above two inward marks)

They put out his eyes. Lack of spiritual discernment. Bound – bondage. Service – becomes a routine – his work. God used him more in his death than in his life.

"Word came AGAIN to Jonah" – Jonah 3:1

Jesus asked Peter more than once – John 21:15

RUTH

'Operation 39' – Lesson 8

This short book of four chapters can be read carefully and thoughtfully in just over half-an-hour. It is a book that you can read right through at one sitting and is such a delightful book that you will want to read it through two or three times.

It is called Ruth because Ruth is the chief character in the story. It is one of the two books in the Bible named after a woman and the only book in the Bible devoted to the history of a woman.

The Book of Ruth is often referred to as the Appendix to The Book of Judges. The events took place 'in the days when the Judges ruled' 1:1, but great is the contrast between this book and the story found in Judges. It indicates that even in the midst of general apostasy and anarchy there were those who were pure and true, lovely and of good report and who had faith in God. The Book has been variously described as like 'an oasis in a desert' or 'a lily in a stagnant pool.'

AUTHORSHIP

This is not stated within the Book but is traditionally assigned to Samuel. 1:1 indicates that the author is looking back to the times of the Judges. 4:22 indicates that it is unlikely to have been written either earlier or later than the times of David. The story presents a vivid picture of the life of the day and as such supports the traditional view that in all probability Samuel wrote it.

HISTORY PERIOD COVERED BY THE WRITING

The story covers a period of just over 10 years (1:1 & 4), within the period when the Judges were over Israel.

DETAILS TO MEMORIZE

KEY WORDS – Redeemed and Restored or Rest through Redemption

KEY VERSES – 1:16-17

NUMBER OF CHAPTERS – 4

OUTSTANDING CHARACTERS – Ruth – Naomi – Boaz – Orpah

Each of these characters is interesting and has spiritual significance. Naomi is typical of a backsliding saint. Orpah represents a sinner who rejects the one way of blessing. Ruth speaks to us of a sinner who believes, makes her choice and is blessed indeed. Boaz may be regarded as a type of Christ. He is referred to as the lord of the harvest – 2:3, the giver of bread – 3:15, the kinsman redeemer – 2:20, the one who gives rest – 3:1, and is the man of wealth. The name Boaz means 'strength;' thus reminding us once again that the Lord is our strength and sufficiency.

The outstanding portrayal of Christ is as the Kinsman-Redeemer, as typified in Boaz.

The Principal Message of the book may be summed up in the following sentence:

Rest through redemption and union with the Redeemer

In this connection it is instructive to note that Elimelech and Naomi forsook the Promised Land and found no rest, but on the other hand Ruth found rest through redemption and union with Boaz. It teaches the important lesson that when the child of God turns to the world there is no rest and that the believer finds that promised rest only when in fellowship and union with the Lord Jesus, the Redeemer. Then and then only do Christians become fruitful and a blessing to others. This is illustrated in this instance in the case of Ruth.

Why is this book in the Scriptures? What is the principal purpose for which is was written?

The story contained in Ruth is so delightful that the principal purpose for which the book was written must not be overlooked. It is an important historic document revealing the founding of the line of David from whence Christ came according to the flesh – 4:18-22. This was of the utmost importance if prophecy concerning the Lord Jesus was to be fulfilled – that He came of the seed of Abraham and of the Royal line of David. This book traces the lineage of David and therefore is an important link in the genealogy of Christ.

If you refer to Matt. 1 you will observe that Ruth is one of five women who appear in the genealogy of our Lord, the others being Tamar, Rahab, Bathsheba and Mary, His earthly mother.

AN ANLYSIS OF THE BOOK IS AS FOLLOWS

Departure to Moab	1:1-5
Return to the land	1:6-22
The Meeting with Boaz	2
Redeemed and United in Marriage	3:1 – 4:22

Another division according to the chapters may be stated as follows:

The Result of Love	1
The Response of Love	2
The Request of Love	3
The Reward of Love	4

Yet a further Analysis centered around the thought of Rest could be:

Rest Forsaken	1:1-5
Rest Desired	1:6-22
Rest Sought	2:1-3
Rest Secured	4:1-22

Never judge the value of a book in Scripture by its length. This is a literary gem, but also it is full of spiritual and typical teaching. A reference to the typical significance of Naomi, Ruth and Boaz has been stated in paragraph beginning "The outstanding portrayal of Christ..."

I SAMUEL

'Operation 39' – Lesson 9

As you read this book right through you will notice that the history contained is presented in the attractive form of biography of the principal characters named later in the notes. Also read Psa. 78:65-72.

POSTION IN THE HEBREW BIBLE

First and Second Samuel originally were one book found in the Section known as 'The Former Prophets.' This book, together with Kings and Chronicles, was divided by the Septuagint translators. They named 1 and 2 Samuel; The First and Second Books of the Kingdoms; 1 and 2 Kings were called "The Third and Fourth Books of the Kingdoms." It was Jerome in the Vulgate who called the four books The First, Second, Third and Fourth Books of the Kings, hence the subtitles in the English Authorized Version.

AUTHORSHIP

The fact that this writing bears the name of Samuel does not necessarily mean it was written by him, but in all probability Samuel or one of his disciples wrote chapters 1 to 24 and 25 to 31 may have been written by Nathan and Gad. See 1 Sam. 10:25 and 1 Chron. 29:29.

HISTORICAL PERIOD COVERED BY THE WRITING

This has variously been set down as covering between 95 and 110 years. There are those who date it 1150 to 1055 B.C. and others who date it from 1110 to 1010 B.C. This period was a transition period in the history of Israel from the Theocracy to the institution of the Monarchy. The narrative of 1 Sam. Extends from the time of Eli (who may have been contemporary with Samson) to the death of Saul and the accession of David to the throne of Israel.

This period was also transitional in another sense. The Warrior-Judges of whom we read in the earlier book of Judges have passed away. Eli was a Priest-Judge and was followed by Samuel, the Prophet-Judge. With him the Period of the Judges ends and the Prophetic Order begins. Prior to this, the Priest had been outstanding in the affairs of the nation. From this time on, the Prophet assumes the greater prominence. It may be helpful to think of the difference between the Priest and Prophet by stating that the Priest was man's representative to God and the Prophet was God's spokesman to man. By the former, the people approached God and the Priest interceded on their behalf. By the Prophet, God drew near to the people and made known His will through the Prophet.

DETAILS TO MEMORIZE

KEY WORD – Kingdom

KEY VERSES – 8:5-9 and 8:19-22. These deal with the national and historic contents of the book.

KEY CHAPTER – 8 – dealing with the demand for the King

OUTSTANDING CHAPTERS – 8; 15; 16; 17

NUMBER OF CHAPTERS – 31

OUTSTANDING CHARACTERS: Eli, Samuel, Saul, David, Jonathan. Each of these characters present an interesting and profitable character study.

Samuel ranks with Moses as one of Israel's greatest leaders. He is often looked upon as the first of the Prophets although there were others prior to Samuel. This no doubt is because he instituted the Schools of the Prophets and laid the foundation of education for Israel as a nation. It was from these training schools that there later arose, under God's direction, the mighty line of Hebrew prophets, the like of which has never been found in any other nation. His ministry was methodical, chapter 7:6-17. He drew up the Constitution of the Kingdom – 10:25. In his prayer life Samuel is a picture of Christ – compare 12:23; Psa. 99:6; Jer. 15:1; Heb. 7:24. Above all, he was an outstanding man of God.

NOTABLE FEATURES

There are several details which are worthy of special note:

1. For the first time in the Bible the title 'The Lord of Hosts' is used. Later it is used approximately 280 times.

2. For the first time the name 'Messiah' is found, being used in 2:10. 'Anointed' is literally Messiah which is the Hebrew form of the Greek word 'Christ.'

3. For the first time the words 'Ichabod' (meaning 'the glory is departed') 4:21 and 'Ebenezer' (meaning 'the stone of help') – 7:12 are used. Here also there is the first use of the familiar phrase 'God save the King' – 10:24. Specially look up and read the context of each of these.

4. In 9:9 you have the first reference to a Prophet being called a 'Seer.' A Prophet is one who had discernment in understanding the Word of the Lord and by reason of this and the anointing of the Holy Spirit was a Seer into and a sharer of the counsels of God.

5. The first reference to Bible Schools! See 10:5 and 19-20

The ministry of the Holy Spirit is emphasized, as for instance in 10:6-9; 11:6; 16:13-18

One of the principal messages of the book may be summed up in the following sentence:

There is a place for prayer in every experience of life.

Particularly note this in the life of Samuel who himself was given to Hannah as an answer to prayer.

It may further be learned from this book that:

Man may change but the purposes and supremacy of the Lord remain unchanged.

This may be illustrated by surveying the different characters and differing response to God's call on the part of Eli, Samuel, Saul and David. Nevertheless the purposes and movement of God continue unaltered.

There are two major tragedies in this book. First, Eli, as an old man, failing to correct and discipline his sons – 2:12. Secondly, Saul's tragic failure. Observe this and make suitable headings to sum up his life story.

ANALYSIS OF CONTENTS

According to the events the book may be divided thus:

| The End of the Theocracy | 1-7 |
| The Beginning of the Monarchy | 8-31 |

The contents are however, best divided around the principal characters and the book lends itself to the following threefold division:

Eli and Samuel	1-17
Samuel and Saul	3-15
Saul and David	16-31

In striking contrast to Saul is David. Observe the references to him and likewise draw up a summary of the ways in which he is described. There is much also in Jonathan's life which is most commendable. The friendship between David and Jonathan should be specially noted. It is one of the greatest friendships of all time.

Who has not been thrilled at the reading of the story in chapter 17?

The outstanding presentation of Christ is as King for here, as in the other historic books, Christ is foreshadowed as the Coming King. In this book it is David who is the man of God's choice. He is anointed King, but lives in rejection while a usurper is on the throne, yet in due time David comes to the Kingdom reminding us that

> Our Lord is now rejected,
> And by the world disowned;
> By the many still neglected,
> And by the few enthroned;
> But soon He'll come in Glory!
> And then He will reign for ever and ever !

II SAMUEL

'Operation 39' – Lesson 10

In addition to reading the whole of this Book through, also read and take particular note of the following Psalms – 23, 25, 26, 37, 38 and 51. If time permits the other Psalms of David could be read with profit in connection with the history of David recorded in this Second Book of Samuel.

See Paragraph 2 of Lesson 9.

Although 1 and 2 Samuel were originally one and the same writing yet the division that has been made is a natural one as The Second Book of Samuel is almost entirely devoted to the history of the reign of David.

The First Book of Samuel records the failure of government in the hands of man's appointed king – Saul. The Second Book of Samuel tells of the success of government in the hands of God's appointed king – David.

HISTORIC PERIOD COVERED BY THE WRITING

Nearly 40 years – that is embracing practically all the reign of David in the eleventh century B.C. During this time the Kingdom reached its greatest extent and highest development. Under the kingship of David it became an important power that had to be reckoned with in the world of its day. It became a prosperous kingdom and laid the foundation of continued prosperity and the glory of the subsequent reign of Solomon.

The same period is dealt with in 1 Chron. 11-29.

AUTHORSHIP

It cannot be stated with certainty but possibly Nathan and Gad who were contemporaries of David – see 1 Chron. 29:29 noting the Revised Version rendering.

DETAILS TO MEMORIZE

KEY WORD – 'Established' This can apply both the Kingdom and to David as King

KEY PHRASE – 'The Lord established David King'

KEY VERSE – 5:12

NUMBER OF CHAPTERS – 24 OUTSTANDING CHARACTERS – David and Joab

The following passages should be specially noted:

- David's Lament over Saul and Jonathan – 1:17-27 called the 'Song of the Bow' – See 1:18 Revised Version. What pathos is to be found in these words! How they reveal the greatness of David's love and heart! Not one word of bitterness against the man who had so often and long sought his life.

- David's declaration contained in 23:1-3. This declaration embraces all the essential elements of the inspiration of the Word of God. It is the Word of God given by the Holy Spirit of God and made available through the words and hand of a man.

- Two parables are used to enforce spiritual lessons – firstly in 12:1-7 by Nathan who was sent by the Lord unto David. In particular note the use of the parable to enforce the spiritual lesson. Nathan's stinging accusation and David's confession before the Lord. Illustrations should be clear and to the point. Alongside this passage read Psalm 51.

- Secondly, note in 14:1-20 the further use of a parable to enforce the spiritual lesson.

- David's great declaration found in 24:24 demands thoughtful consideration. It is challenging and searching to say the least.

The Message of the Book may be summed up in the following two phrases;

'Wait patiently on the Lord'

David had to wait many years for the fulfillment of the Lord's promises, but his faith never faltered and in due time he came to the kingdom – 5:1-3

'Be sure your sin will find you out'

David, the man of privilege, was not however given the privilege to sin and that which was done secretly was laid bare and there followed great suffering and distress to David and his family.

ANALYSIS OF CONTENTS

		Period
David, King of Judah in Hebron	1:1 – 4:11	7 years
David, King of all Israel in Jerusalem	5:1 – 24:25 (and I Kings 2:11)	33 years
• The King's Triumph	1:1 – 10:19	
• The King's Troubles	11:1-20:22	
• The King's Testimony	22:1-24:25	

The outstanding prophecy of the Book is concerned with the Davidic Covenant; that is, the establishment of the Throne of David and the Everlasting Kingship – 7:11-17. Thus, the outstanding portrayal of Christ in this book is as the Coming King of which David is a foreshadowing.

It will be profitable at this stage to trace the development of the prophecies relating to the coming of the Messiah:

Genesis 3:15	Given approximately 4,000 B.C.
Genesis 9:26	" " 2, 300 B.C.
Genesis 12:1-3	" " 2, 000 B.C.
Genesis 26:3-4	" "
28:13-14	
49:10	" " 1,800 B.C.
I Samuel 7:11-17	" " 1,000 B.C.

The promise is not limited to David and his sons – Solomon and Nathan by Bathsheba. From Solomon descended Joseph, the legal father of Christ – Matt. 1:6 and 16. From Nathan descended Mary, the virgin mother of Christ according to the flesh – Luke 3:23 and 31. Thus it is seen that Christ was the Son of David both legally and organically for His earthy parents both sprang out of David. Hence, from the time of Nathan's prophecy the coming Messiah is the Son of David.

The details concerning David found in this book give much food for thought, encouragement and admonition. To a considerable extent the book deals with David's personal history and his attitude 'before the Lord.' With this in mind take particular note of David's confidence in and dependence upon the Lord – 2:1; 5:3; 6:6-21; 7:18; 8:6-14; 12:16; 15:25-26; 16:12; 21:1; 24:17; 24:24-25

Observe also that although greatly privileged, David was not exempt from the harvest of his sin – see Gal. 6:7.

Further note David's gracious dealings with Mephibosheth. It is an illustration of the grace of our Lord Jesus.

It was during David's reign that the Kingdom of Israel became powerful but even more important than this, it was by his establishing Jerusalem as the central Capital of the Kingdom that Jerusalem came to occupy the place that henceforth it did in the thought, worship and writings of the Hebrew people. Being a sweet singer and composer himself, he encouraged the development of poetry and music and gave birth to the Psalms which had a profound influence upon Hebrew literature as expressed in the writings of the prophets.

He is referred to as 'shepherd of Israel' in 5:2 and is the first to be described 'the Lord's anointed' – see 1:14, 16 and 21; 2:4 and 7; 3:39; 5:3 and 17; 19:10; 22:51.

1 KINGS

'Operation 39' – Lesson 11

The twenty-two chapters of this book are best read without interruption but if this is not possible then read the book through according to the two main divisions given below. In addition read Psalm 72. The parallel passage in the Chronicles is found in 2 Chron. 1:1 – 21:1.

As in the case of the other two historical books (1 and 2 Samuel and 1 and 2 Chronicles) the First and Second Books of Kings were originally one book. They deal with the lives of the Kings and the story of the Kingdom. The Book was divided in two by the Septuagint translators and called by them the Third and Fourth Books of the Kingdoms. In the Vulgate they are called the Third and Fourth Books of the Kings. Hence the subtitles in the English Authorized Version. The reason for the division was on account of the Greek language demanding more room than the original Hebrew and the Greek translation would have been unwieldy on one scroll.

In the Hebrew Bible, 1 and 2 Kings are included in the section 'Former Prophets.' They contain history with a meaning and tell forth the message of God. They are, therefore, prophetic in the true and Biblical meaning of that term; namely, to tell forth the message of God rather than to foretell the future.

The historic period covered by 1 Kings is about 120 years and follows on from the end of the second Book of Samuel. It includes the closing days of David, covers the reign of Solomon of 40 years and then gives the history of the other kings who reigned after the Kingdom was divided in Judah and Israel to approximately 850 B.C.

2 Samuel and 1 Kings cover the Golden Age of Hebrew history. Israel was a world power in the later part of the reign of David and during the reign of Solomon. Contemporary history shows that Egypt's power was waning. Assyria and Babylon were weak. It was also the contemporary age of Homer in Greece but note 4:30-34 where it speaks of the wisdom of Solomon and of those who came to learn of him.

Compare 1 and 2 Kings. 1 Kings opens with the glory of the Kingdom. 2 Kings closes with the Kingdom in ruins.

According to Hebrew tradition the author was Jeremiah the Prophet. It is evident from the reference in 8:8 that the Temple was still standing. It will also be seen that official sources for documents have been referred to by the author – 11:41; 14:29; 14:19 – the Book of the Acts of Solomon, the Book of the Chronicles of the Kings of Judah, the Book of the Chronicles of the Kings of Israel. The language and purpose of the writing which we now know as 1 and 2 Kings, is such that they point to having been written by one writer.

The following Scriptures make an interesting comparison with passages in Jeremiah:

1 Kings 8:51	Jeremiah 11:4
1 Kings 9:8-9	Jeremiah 22:8-9
2 Kings 21: 12	Jeremiah 19:2-3
2 Kings 25:30	Jeremiah 52:34

MEMORIZE THE FOLLOWING DETAILS

THREE KEY WORDS convey the story of the Book – Glory – Disruption – Decline

KEY VERSES – 10:4-9; 11:11; 12:19 and 24; 14:25-28

NUMBER OF CHAPTERS: 22

There are three outstanding chapters as follows:

Solomon's Prayer at the Dedication of the Temple 8

THE BEST OF CAPERNWRAY

Elijah's Stand for the Lord on Mount Carmel 18

Revealing the Tactics of the Adversary of the People of God 20

OUTSTANDING CHARACTERS – Solomon the King and Elijah the Prophet

A BRIEF ANALYSIS OF THE BOOK IS AS FOLLOWS

I. The United Kingdom – chapters 1-11 Period – 40 years

II. The Kingdom Divided – chapters 12 – 24 Period – 80 years

A fuller Analysis follows:

I. Solomon Established on the Throne	1:1 – 2:46
II. The Glory of the Kingdom	3:1 – 11:43
A. Solomon's Wisdom and Wealth	Chaps. 3 and 4
B. Solomon's Works	5:1 – 9:9
C. Solomon's Fame	9:10 – 10:29
D. Solomon's Waywardness	11
III. The Disruption of the Kingdom	12:1-24
IV. The Decline of the Kingdom	12:25-22:53
A. The Apostasy of the Northern Kingdom under Jeroboam	12:25-53
B. The Apostasy of the Southern Kingdom under Rehoboam	14:21-24
C. Judah and Israel at war	

One of the main messages of the book is to teach the failure of government by man in contrast to the persistent, unfailing government of God.

This is shown by the failure of the Autocracy of Solomon and Rehoboam and the Democracy of Jeroboam followed by the intrigues of others, all ending in failure. Under man's government the narrative leads downward from glory to spiritual apostasy and material loss.

The persistent and unfailing government of God is revealed as He declares his sovereignty through the voice of the prophet, for instance, in particular note 22:19. As you read this book observe the references to prophets some of whom are named and others are left unnamed. The overruling of God is revealed through His blessing obedience and bringing punishment and chastisement to the disobedient.

Observe the following three details:

- Prophecy by an unnamed man of God in 13:2. It came to pass three hundred years later – recorded in 2 Kings 23:16-18

- Joshua's prediction concerning Jericho found in Joshua 6:26 is fulfilled in 1 Kings 16:34

- The City of Samaria to which reference is made on many occasions in both the Old and the New Testament was built by Omri, King of Israel – 16:24

The principal portrayal of Christ in this book is as the coming King. Solomon in all his glory foreshadows the reign of Christ on earth. Also as builder of the Temple Solomon typifies Christ, who through the Eternal Spirit is building the living Temple, the Church of God. See such Scriptures as Eph. 2:19-22; 1 Tim. 3:15; 1 Pet. 2:5

Also, Solomon departed from the faith and conduct of David, his father, and although greatly gifted intellectually and receiving wisdom in answer to his prayer, he later developed great wickedness and acted most foolishly.

Elijah the Prophet is expressly referred to by the Lord as foreshadowing John the Baptist – Matt. 11:14; 17:1-30; Mark 9:11-30. Elijah is referred to more than any other prophet in the New Testament. He was a man of courage, faith and zeal. As you read of him, try to recall similar incidents in the life and ministry of John the Baptist. The account of Elijah's ministry is found in 1 Kings 17 to 2 Kings 2.

In this book also you read of the call of Elisha in 19:19-21. It is the story of a wealthy young man, responding to the call of God, through a servant of God. Amidst apostasy, declension and disaster God has His man for the hour; Elijah and those who will respond to His call – Elisha.

2 KINGS

'Operation 39' – Lesson 12

In addition to reading this book right through also read the Book of Lamentations. The parallel history found in the Book of Chronicles is 2 Chron. 21 to 36.

You are referred to Lesson 11, Paragraph 2 for as it is there stated 1 and 2 Kings were originally one book and in the Hebrew Bible occupy a place in the section known as 'The Former Prophets.'

In 2 Kings there are again references to various official sources and documents on which the details have been taken; namely, The Book of the Acts of Solomon and seventeen references to the Chronicles of the Kings of Israel; fifteen references to the Chronicles of the Kings of Judah. These references are not of course to the books known as 1 and 2 Chronicles in the Old Testament for these latter were written by Ezra at a considerably later date after the captivity in Babylon. The references in 2 Kings refer to official State Documents.

MEMORIZE THE FOLLOWING DETAILS

KEY WORD – Downfall

KEY PHRASE – 'According to the Word of the Lord'

KEY VERSES – 17:23 and 24:2

NUMBER OF CHAPTERS – 25

OUTSTANDING CHAPTERS – 19 and 20, but several others also have their special significance.

OUTSTANDING CHARACTERS – Prophets Elijah and Elisha and the good kings of Judah; namely, Hezekiah and Josiah.

Elijah is translated by the Lord, Whom he had served so faithfully.

Elisha, of whose call you read in the First Book of Kings had a ministry which lasted probably 66 years. Attention is focused on his miracles and it will be seen that his deeds brought healing and blessing. His ministry followed that of Elijah. In the New Testament, Elijah is spoken of as a type or foreshadowing of John the Baptist. It will therefore be seen that the ministry of Elisha is typical of that of the Lord Jesus. Pay special attention to Elisha's miracles and deeds recorded in the following Scriptures: 2:14,21,24; 3:20; 4:1-6,16,17,35,41,43; 5:10 and 27; 6:6,17,18,20; 13:21.

In the Books of Kings, Chronicles and Isaiah, Hezekiah has more space devoted to his life than any other of the kings of the divided Kingdom. There was Revival in his reign – 2 Kings 18:4-5 and the two outstanding chapters, 19 and 20 deal with important incidents in Hezekiah's life.

Josiah was Hezekiah's great grandson and led a great Revival recorded in 22:8 onwards. It was in the thirteenth year of the reign of Josiah that Jeremiah's prophetic ministry commenced.

BRIEF ANALYSIS OF THE BOOK

The Closing Ministry of Elijah	1:1 – 2:11
The Ministry of Elisha	2:12 – 13:21
The Fall and Captivity of Israel	13:22 – 17:41
The Fall and Captivity of Judah	18:1 – 25:30

The historic period covered by 2 Kings is approximately 300 years, possibly from 896 to 586 B.C. Within this period the Hebrew 'writing' Prophets wrote and prophesied and their books in the Old Testament can be understood the better when read in connection with the historic background. At a later stage in this course when dealing with the prophetic books reference will be made back to the appropriate passages in the historic books. There were also many outstanding 'Oral' Prophets, the chief of whom were Elijah and Elisha.

The contemporary history of this period shows that the power of Egypt was on the wane and Syria became powerful to be followed later by the rise of Assyria from the reign of Ahab onward. The capital of Assyria was Nineveh and it became the World power under Shalmeneser who took Israel into captivity – 2 Kings 17:21-22. Sennacherib laid siege to Jerusalem in the reign of Hezekiah. Later Babylon recovered its independence from Assyria and rose to power. In 612 B.C. Nabopolassar took Nineveh and in 6-5 B.C. his famous son, Nebuchadnezzar gained a decisive victory over the Egyptian forces at Carchemish and Babylon became the world power. Judah was taken into captivity to Babylon by Nebuchadnezzar. The fall of Jerusalem is dated 586 B.C

In contemplating 1 and 2 Kings as it was originally; namely, one book it will be seen that the narrative opens with the man of God's choice, David, coming to the throne and concludes with the King of Babylon subjugating the Kingdom. It tells of the preparations for and the building of the Temple and concludes with Jerusalem destroyed and the Temple burned.

The principal message of this book is a continuation of that found in the First Book of Kings revealing the power of the Lord upon the Eternal Throne in contrast to the failure of the government of the earthly king.

This book is particularly rich in its contents and lends itself to much spiritual application, as for instance, the miracles of Elisha already enumerated above. A study of the following phrases which are used with frequency in the narrative will be most profitable:

- "The man of God" is to be found in this book more times than in any book in the Bible. Generally it is with reference to the prophets who were God's witnesses and mouthpieces during days of general departure from God. There are 35 or 36 such references.

- "The Word of the Lord" and similar expressions such as "The Word the Lord hath spoken" all used 24 times – 1:17; 4:44; 7:1 & 16; 9:26 & 36; 10:10; 14:25; 15:12; 19:21; 20:4; 23:2,3,16; 24:2.

- "The anger and wrath of the Lord" revealing His displeasure against and judgment on disobedience – 13:3; 17:18; 22:13 & 17; 23:26; 24:20.

- "He did that which was evil in the sight of the Lord." The writer has the practice of giving a verdict on each King's reign. 21 times over this expression is to be found.

- "He did that which was right in the sight of the Lord," again revealing the writer's practice of giving a verdict on the King's reign. This expression is however only found eight times in comparison with the opposite statement above.

Consideration of the above phrases reveals something of the principal purpose of the Book. God sent the man of God to warn the people and to bring them back to the Lord. Their message was one with divine authority. They spoke the Word of the Lord and when this was rejected His anger and wrath was revealed against the disobedient and they were delivered into the hands of their enemies.

It is worthy to note the sovereignty of the Lord in preserving the royal line of David – 9:1-3 and in preserving and making available once again the Law given through Moses – 22:8-20

The Northern Kingdom, Israel, had 19 kings belonging to 9 different dynasties. All of these Kings without exception were bad.

The Southern Kingdom, Judah, had 19 kings and 1 queen. All the kings belonged to the dynasty of the House of David, some of whom were good and others were bad. As you read the book you will note how the standard set by David was applied to the Kings of Judah and the evil example set by Jeroboam, the son of Nabat, casts its shadows across the Kings of Israel. In 1 and 2 Kings it is said approximately 25 times that he sinned or made others to sin.

Every believer is casting a shadow or setting an example – for good or for evil.

1 CHRONICLES

'Operation 39' – Lesson 13

Have you ever previously read through the First and Second Books of Chronicles? These two book are often sadly neglected by Christians and now is your opportunity if never before to settle down and read through for this study of the First Book Chronicles.

In the Hebrew Bible, 1 and 2 Chronicles are one book and as in the case of the Books of Samuel and kings, it was divided by the Greek translators. They come at the end of the Hebrew Bible, that is, in the third division known as the Hagiographer. This division is also referred to as the Psalms – Luke 24:44 by reason of the fact that the Book of Psalms was the first book in the section and also the longest.

The Hebrew title for the book is 'Journal' or more strictly 'Words of Day.' In the Septuagint the title is 'Omissions' or 'Things omitted.' This latter title suggests that the Books of the Chronicles was supplementary to those of the Kings and while they do, of course, include material not found in the other historical books there is a special purpose for the further record.

The name 'Chronicles' comes to us from Jerome's translation in the fourth Century A.D., that is from the Vulgate.

There are references in 1 and 2 Chronicles to several sources which have been consulted and from which information has been extracted. Write out a list of these. They are to be found in the following references: 1 Chron. 9:1; 29:29; 2 Chron. 9:29; 12:15; 16:11; 20:34; 24:27; 25:26; 26:22; 28:26; 32:32; 33:19.

To refer to these sources will not in any way detract from Divine inspiration of the writing for the Spirit of God would have directed the author in his compilation from these records. It is usually thought that the writer was Ezra, the Scribe. This is the Hebrew tradition and there is to be observed close similarity of style between the Books of the Chronicles and Ezra-Nehemiah. Indeed there are those who believe that they may have originally been one complete writing. The Books, Ezra and Nehemiah continue with the historic narrative where Chronicles finishes. Compare 2 Chronicles 36:22 and 23 with Ezra 1:1-2.

From 6:15 and 9:1 the writer is looking back on the captivity and 3:17-24 brings the writing down to Ezra and Nehemiah's time. In 2 Chron. 36:22-23 Cyrus' edict is also in the past. This supports the tradition that Ezra wrote the Chronicles shortly after the return from the Babylonian captivity. The number of Aramaisms which are introduced into the Hebrew text also support the view that the writing was post-exilic. In Chronicles, as in Ezra, there is the emphasis on genealogies and temple worship.

1 Chronicles commences with Adam and terminates with the coming of Solomon to the throne; in other words a period of about 3,000 years. 2 Chronicles continues the story to the decree of Cyrus in 586 B.C., thus the two books (remember originally one writing) cover the history of a period of not less than 3,500 years. On this fact alone you are left to judge whether or not the Chronicles demand special study.

One of the chief objects in the genealogical tables in chapters 1 to 9 is to trace David's line back to Adam and on down to the Babylonian captivity. Observe also the prominence given to the genealogy of the Priests.

In keeping with the message and purpose of the Book, prominence is given to the ordering of the temple service and other Levitical details.

MEMORIZE THE FOLLOWING DETAILS

KEY WORD – Worship

KEY PHRASE – 'The Lord reigneth'

L.A.T. VAN DOOREN

KEY VERSES – 16:31; 29:11-13; 29:20

NUMBER OF CHAPTERS - 29

OUTSTANDING CHAPTERS

- Containing David's Psalm of thanksgiving – 16

- Containing David's Testimony concerning God and charge to Solomon – 28

- Dealing with David's gifts for the Temple. His further Psalm of Adoration for the Lord and the willing offering both of princes and people – 29

There are two outstanding characters in this book:

Saul – the narrator deals with his life in one chapter because it was a wasted life which brought no glory to God.

David – the man after God's own heart on the other hand has ten chapters or so devoted to his activities. Then there are a further 8 or 9 chapters dealing with the ordering of the Temple Service, preparation of materials, etc., all of which was carried out at David's instigation. His was a life which despite its faults and its sin, sought to glorify God and fulfill His purpose.

THE FOLLOWING IS A SIMPLE ANALYSIS

Genealogies from Adam to David	1-9
The Death of Saul	10
The Exploits of David	11-20
The Preparations for the Temple	21-29

It has already been pointed out in these notes that Chronicles deals with Biblical history already recorded elsewhere in earlier books and the question might well be sked as to why there is this repetition of historic matter. In answer to this question it should be remembered that it was written shortly after the return from captivity. Therefore, one of its prime purposes was to encourage the people and to remind them of their glorious spiritual heritage and so not only reestablish the worship of Jehovah but also bring the people to a true recognition of God's presence in the midst. It was also necessary to remind the people of God that in reality they were a Theocracy, even if not so in earthly and outward appearance. So we discover that this book was written to enforce great spiritual truths which can be summarized as follows:

- The Lord reigns – in the genealogies He is seen selecting men not according to birthright and human privilege but according to that obedience which formulates character.

- The Lord is ever active in the affairs of men, therefore recognize His activity.

- Magnify the Lord and honor God with the central place whether it be in national or individual life.

There are certain noteworthy differences in the account of Kings and 1 Chron. And these are intended to convey points of spiritual importance:

Ishbosheth – the son of Saul (2 Sam. 2:8) is called Esh-Baal in 1 Chron. 8:33. His name means 'man of Baal' and suggests that his father, Saul, had at the time of his birth apostatized and had begun to worship Baal. This will help us to understand something of the tragic failure of Saul as King.

Compare 1 Sam. 31 with 1 Chron. 10:1-44. It will be seen that the emphasis is on the Lord's judgment and therefore it must be recognized that the Philistines were the instruments which God chose to use to execute His judgment on Saul.

Compare 2 Sam. 6 with 1 Chron. 13-16. It will be noticed in the latter writing that there are three chapters as compared to one in the Book of Samuel dealing with the return of the Ark. Also, here you have the reason for Uzziah's death and David's confession of his negligence in carrying out God's Word.

You do not read in 1 Chon. of any reference to David's sin regarding Uriah, the Hittite. This suggests a glorious spiritual truth; when God forgives, He forgets and promises to remember our iniquities no more.

There is reference to David's sin of numbering in 1 Chron., but this is only on account of the act that it led to the purchase of the Temple site. In 1 Chron. 21:1 the true instigator of the sin is revealed. It was Satan who moved David and this detail is not given in the earlier writing.

There are one or two numerical details which differ in these records and that of earlier writings. For instance, compare 2 Sam. 24:24 and 1 Chron. 21:25. The reference in Samuel relates to the purchase of the Altar site and the reference in Chronicles is in connection with the purchase of the whole farm of Ornah (also called Araunah) which became the future Temple site. Similar points would no doubt be clear if we had further information. It has been ably said that the former historic records survey events from an earthly point of view whereas in this book they are surveyed from a spiritual and divine viewpoint. In this connection it is noteworthy that the writer has more to say on the Temple and its ritual than of the wars of the kings.

After the genealogies it will be seen that Chronicles deals solely with the kingdom of Judah because it is dealing with the chosen line of David from whence was to spring the Messiah whereas the Books of Samuel and Kings are concerned with the history of the kingdoms of Judah and Israel.

Your attention is drawn once again to chapter 29 with its emphasis upon the people of God giving willingly for the work of the Lord. May this be true of each student of these notes. Offer willingly and you will have the double joy of seeing others following your example and likewise offering willingly unto the Lord.

2 CHRONICLES

'Operation 39' – Lesson 14

In the Second Book of Chronicles you have thirty-six chapters to be read through. Do so carefully and prayerfully. God, who inspired the writer and overruled so that the writing was included in the Canon of Scripture, had a purpose in setting these things on record and preserving them for His people. They are written for our admonition – Romans 15:4; 2 Tim. 3:16-17; 2 Pet. 1:19-21.

You are referred to Lesson 13, paragraphs 2 and 3 for the introductory details of 2 Chronicles. They are very much the same as for 1 Chronicles, but remember, as it has already been pointed out in the previous lesson, that 1 and 2 Chronicles were originally one book.

The present book continues the history of Judah to the return under the decree of Cyrus. The full period covered by 1 and 2 Chronicles extends from Adam until 586 B.C.

The further history of the people of God is continued in the Books of Ezra, Esther and Nehemiah in the Old Testament.

MEMORIZE THE FOLLOWING DETAILS

It is easier to sum up the message of the book in a Key Phrase rather than one Key Word.

KEY PHRASE – 'Seek the Lord'

KEY VERSE – 7:14

(The verses dealing with 'Seek the Lord' are set out in a later paragraph)

NUMBER OF CHAPTERS – 36

There are several themes running through this book and it would be possible to choose different verses or groups of verses to illustrate these. For instance, take as the theme:

Devotion to God Degraded into formalism leading to Decline and Departure from God and so bringing about Destruction from the hand of the Lord.

Key Verses illustrating this are as follows: 5:13-14; 7:1-2; 12:9 & 11; 33:1-2; 36:14-20.

The book does not lend itself to a very close Analysis but a brief Analysis is as follows:

The Reign of Solomon	1 – 9
• His worship	1:1-6 and Chap. 6
• His wisdom	1:7-13 and 9:1-12
• His work of building the temple	3:1 – 6:11
• His wealth	9:13-28
The Kings of Judah	10:1 – 36:13
The Destruction of Jerusalem and the Captivity	36:5-21
The Decree of Cyrus	36:22-23

A further Analysis according to the Theme given in the paragraph above regarding themes could be set out as follows:

Devotion to the Lord	1 – 9
Decline from the Lord	10 – 23
Departure from the Lord	24 – 32
Denial of and Destruction from the Lord	33 – 36

The outstanding chapters are:

Chapter 6 – containing Solomon's truly spiritual prayer at the Consecration of the Temple

Chapters on Revival - 15; 17-19; 23-24; 29-30 and 34

Although the analysis above emphasizes the departure from the Lord, yet it will be seen within this book that there is recorded five great revivals under the following kings:

	Chapters
Asa	15
Jehoshaphat (In one sense Jehoshaphat carried on the work of revival which commenced under his father Asa)	17 and 19
Joash	23 – 24
Hezekiah	29 – 30
Josiah	34

There were distinctive features of these five great religious movements. Observe them in your reading.

The three outstanding messages of 2 Chron. are all reemphasized in this writing. You will recall in the notes for 1 Chron. that the message of the Book was set out as follows:

- The Lord reigns – in the genealogies He is seen selecting man not according to birthright and human privilege but according to that obedience which formulates character.

- The Lord is ever active in the affairs of men therefore recognizes His activity.

- Magnify the Lord and honor God with the central place whether it be in national or individual life.

If ever there was a book which warned God's people of the danger of declining into a merely outward and formal observance of religious ordinances it is this book. It also reveals the powerlessness of formal religion. An interesting comparison is to be found in Acts 21 where the church at Jerusalem is said to number many thousands and yet was powerless because it was zealous for outward form and ceremony.

The outstanding portrayal of Christ in this book is in the Temple. Christ spoke of His body as the Temple – John 2:19-21. In this connection observe Solomon's six references to prayer in chapter 6 and his oft repeated petition that if those in need were to turn to this place (the Temple) they should receive an answer. Thus, he said in type what our Lord said in actual truth – John 14:13-14.

The differences between the Books of Kings and 2 Chronicles are in accordance with the spiritual emphasis of the latter writing and are as follows:

Compare 2 Chronicles 8:11 with 1 Kings 7:8. It is Chronicles that tells us that Solomon though marrying an idolatrous wife would not permit her to reside in the Holy City.

Compare 2 Chronicles 11:15 and 13:15 and 20 with 1 Kings 14:19-20.

In 2 Chronicles 13 we read of Abijah's address and prayer to God which is not referred to in Kings but where his reign is portrayed as wholly bad.

In 2 Chronicles there are three chapters – 29-31 – dealing with the revival under Hezekiah whereas in 2 Kings 18 it occupies only three verses; namely 14 to 16. On the other hand, his military exploits which are emphasized in 2 Kings are passed over in only two or three verses in 2 Chronicles. In 2 Chronicles Uzziah's reign of 52 years occupies 2 verses; namely, 26:21-23. Likewise Manasseh's reign of 55 years – 33:1-20. It is in 2 Chronicles that we read of Manasseh's repentance and return to God – 2 Chron. 33:11-13.

Observe the following Scriptures. It would be wise to underline them in our study Bible:

- 'Seek the Lord' – This phrase is found repeatedly – 7:14; 14:4 & 7; 15:2,4,12,13,15; 17:4; 19:3; 20:3-4; 22:9; 26:5; 30:19; 31:21; 34:3. Contrast 12:14 and 16:12.

- There is frequent reference to prayer and the need to rely upon the Lord – 1:1; ch. 6; 13:18; 14:6 & 11; 15:9; 20:27; 26:6-7; 27:6; 32:8 & 22. Contrast 24:24; 28:6 & 19.

- In connection with the above two series of Scriptures your attention is drawn once again to 20:20.

A quiet, thoughtful study of these references leads you right to the heart of the message of the book. Seek the Lord! Believe and obey Him! Serve and love Him with the whole heart and you are on the high road to spiritual blessing and victorious living! For the child of God this will mean full satisfaction and fruitful living for the Lord. Compare 20:27.

HISTORICAL BACKGROUND - PREPARATORY TO THE STUDY OF THE BOOKS OF EZRA, NEHEMIAH AND ESTHER

'Operation 39' – Intro. Lesson to Lessons 15-17

The three books of Ezra, Nehemiah and Esther deal with the return of the Children of Israel from the Babylonian Captivity and their reestablishment in the Land. They complete the historical section of the Old Testament and are referred to as being post-exilic. Incidentally, there are also three books of Prophecy which were written at the same period; namely, Haggai, Zechariah and Malachi.

The Books Ezra, Nehemiah and Esther cover a period of just over 100 years from 537 B.C. to 432 B.C.

During this period of Israel's history there were three outstanding events:

- The Return from Captivity in Babylon
- The Rebuilding of the Temple in Jerusalem
- The Reestablishment of National life in the Promised Land

Within this period of history there were the following personalities and work:

First Period	537-516 B.C.	21 years	Sheshbazzar, that is Zerubbabel was Governor of the land. Joshua, the son of Jozadah was High Priest. The Temple was rebuilt. Haggai's and Zechariah's Prophetic ministry.
Second Period	516-458 B.C.	58 years	No reference is made to this period in the books of Ezra or Nehemiah. It was during this time that the events of the book of Esther took place.
Third Period	458-432 B.C.	26 years	Ezra the Priest and Scribe exercised his ministry. Nehemiah was governor during the latter part of the period from 445 B.C. The walls of Jerusalem were rebuilt and the City fortified. Malachi's prophetic ministry.

The Book of Ezra contains an account of the first and part of the third of the above periods.

The Book of Esther fits in historically in the otherwise blank second period. As near as can be stated, Esther was Queen of Persian in 478 and the suggested date of deliverance from massacre was 473 B.C. The Book of Nehemiah gives an account of events in the third period.

It is helpful to remember that there were two major returns of the Children of Israel from Babylon:

- The First at the Decree of Cyrus – 537. This took place under Zerubbabel – read Ezra 2, 64-69 wherein the numbers of those returning are given; namely, 42,360 Jews; 7,337 servants; 200 singers, etc.

- The Second at the Decree of Artaxerxes Longimanus – 457 B.C. This was under the leadership of Ezra. 1,754 men returned.

In 445 B.C. Nehemiah returned to the Land at the authority of Artaxerxes, taking with him a small army escort.

EZRA

'Operation 39' – Lesson 15

It will not take long to read the Book of Ezra through without interruption, but if you are unable to do this then you are asked to read it in the two main sections given below. Also read the following passages of Jeremiah – 18:1-10; 25:11-14; 29:10-14 and Lamentations 3:31-33. Compare 2 Chronicles 36:22-23 with Ezra 1:1-4. Read Psalm 119.

In the Hebrew Bible this Book is found in the section known as the Hagiographer or Psalms and is one Book with that of Nehemiah.

The Historic Period covered by the writing is from 537-457 B.C.; that is 80 years. During this time there was the return of the main party of the children of Israel from exile in Babylon following the Decree of Cyrus in 537 B.C. The numbers of them returning are given in Ezra 2:64-69. Later there was the return of a further remnant of the Children of Israel under Ezra in 457 B.C.

Between chapters 6 and 7 there is a period of 58 years and it was during this time that the events recorded in the Book of Esther took place.

It is usually thought that <u>Ezra was the author of this Book and also of the Book of Nehemiah</u>. Both Books contain quotations from various official records, documents and letters and are therefore almost as much a compilation as a writing. The Book of Ezra reveals unity of authorship throughout and it is not inconsistent with the writing of a Scribe that Ezra should be referred to in the third person in certain sections of the book.

Ezra was a great-grandson of Hilkiah the High Priest – 7:1 and 2 Kings 22:8. He was also a direct descendant of Aaron 7:1-5. It is thought that it was principally due to Ezra that The Great Synagogue was organized, which was a council of leading Jews governing religious matters. This body was primarily responsible for the reconstruction of Temple worship and religious life and also had considerable influence in settling the Canon of the Old Testament Scriptures. Ezra was an outstanding expositor of the Word of God. His great mission and desire was to bring the Word of God to the people. In addition to writing this book and that of Nehemiah and 1 and 2 Chronicles it is usually considered that he was the author of Psalm 119, every verse of which speaks of the Word of God. You should frequently read this Psalm.

MEMORIZE THE FOLLOWING DETAILS

KEY WORDS – Restoration and Separation

KEY PHRASE – Reconstruction according to the Word of the Lord

KEY Verses – 1:2; 3:2; 6:14; 6:18; 7:10; 9:10; 10:5

NUMBER OF CHAPTERS – 10

The Lord is revealed as the Restorer of His people. In this connection also refer to the passage in Jeremiah 18:1-10. The Lord is the Divine Potter who makes again another vessel for His use and glory according to His Will.

By reason of Ezra's emphasis upon the Word of God, the Book is a powerful message revealing the place and power of the Word of God in the life of the people of God.

Observe the following references to God's Word: 1:1; 3:2; 6:14; 6:18; 7:10; 7:6; 7:14; 9:4; 10:3 & 5. How many different titles or descriptive phrases are given to God's Word? You should make a note of these.

The following is an Analysis of the Book:

The Return from Captivity under Zerubbabel	1:1 – 6:22
• Decree of Cyrus	1
• Return	2
• Reconstruction	3
• Samaritan opposition and Work stopped	4
• Decree of Darius	5
• Completion of the Temple and Observance of Passover	6
The Return from Captivity under Ezra	7:1 – 10:44
• Proclamation of Artaxerxes	7
• Ezra's intercession and Reformation of the People	9-10

It is within the Book of Ezra that two of the Aramaic portions of the Old Testament are to be found; namely, 4:8 - 6:18 and 7:12-26. These passages contain letters and decrees of Persian kings. Aramaic was the official language of diplomatic correspondence at this period of history.

It is worthy of note that there are references to seven different kings and three world empires; namely the Assyrian, Babylonian and Medo-Persian Empires.

Reference has already been made, but your attention is drawn again, to the emphasis on the Word of God and its place in the National, Social and Spiritual life of the people. The Word of God has its application to every department of life.

It will be remembered that when Israel came out of Egypt all Israel came out, whereas at the time of the Decree of Cyrus only those whose spirit was stirred up to go came out of Babylon – 1:5. God is still looking for those among His people who are prepared to forsake 'Babylonish comforts' and to be separate from the things of the world and live in the place of His appointment. The Book does therefore possess a very powerful plan to the backslider to return to the place of blessing, to rebuild the altar which speaks of renewed spiritual cleansing and dedication and to rebuild the Temple which speaks of witness. It is only thus that God can be truly served.

The following passages deserve special attention and noting:

The Decree of Cyrus – 1:2-4

The Erection of the Altar and laying of the Temple Foundation – 3:1-13

References to Haggai, Zechariah – 5:1-2 and 6:14

The Letter of Darius – 6:1-12

Ezra's Prayer – 9:5-15

QUESTIONS ON THE BOOK OF EZRA

1. State the period covered by the Books of Ezra, Nehemiah and Esther and the three outstanding events of that time.

2. Name three outstanding prophets of this period.

3. Give the number of chapters in the Book of Ezra and sum up the Book in one or two key words and a key phrase.

4. Relate the Book of Esther to the historic period covered by the Book of Ezra.

5. What is one of the outstanding characteristics of Ezra's life and ministry?

6. What passage in the Book of Jeremiah may be likened to God's dealings with His people Israel at this time?

7. Divide the Book into two sections.

NEHEMIAH

'Operation 39' – Lesson 16

You are about to study a thrilling book of thirteen chapters and will want to read it through without interruption. If possible, read it more than once. The Book of the Prophet Malachi deals with the latter part of Nehemiah's rule in Jerusalem. It will be helpful also to read Malachi during the study of Nehemiah.

Nehemiah and Ezra were originally counted as one book and in the Vulgate are called 1 and 2 Esdras and in the Septuagint are known as Esdras, but not to be confused with the Apocryphal First Esdras. Nehemiah, in the Hebrew Bible, is found in the Hagiographa or Psalms.

It is important to know the historic background of this book. It will be recalled that after the Children of Israel had been 70 years in captivity in Babylon, Cyrus conquered the Babylonian Empire and issued the decree enabling he Children of Israel to return to the Promised Land. This return took place in two main stages. The first was under Zerubbabel in the year 537 B.C. when the Temple was rebuilt and certain reforms carried out. The second was when Ezra the Scribe returned in 458 B.C. Ezra was a Priest and Scribe and concerned himself with preaching the Word of God and thus seeking to bring the people back to the true worship of the Lord. A small escort accompanied Nehemiah in 445 B.C. These details may be summarized as follows:

| Zerubbabel's return to the Promised Land – 537 B.C. | The Temple rebuilt | Religious Reforms |

Ezra returns – 458 B.C.	The People taught the Word of God	Ethical Reforms
Nehemiah returns – 445 B.C.	The walls of Jerusalem rebuilt and the City reestablished and refortified	Civil Reforms

The Principal difference between the Books of Ezra and Nehemiah is that in the first the emphasis is on the Ecclesiastical aspect and in Nehemiah the emphasis is on the Civil point of view. Hence, the former emphasizes the rebuilding of the Temple and the institution of Temple worship whereas the latter deals with the rebuilding of the Walls of Jerusalem.

Nehemiah's second mission to Jerusalem is dated 432 B.C. but his total administration is said to have covered a much longer period. With this book, the history of the Old Testament ceases.

In reading the book it will be observed that a good deal of it is written in the first person and therefore must be the writing of Nehemiah. It is however thought that Ezra the Scribe was the compiler of the book. If this is so, he must have quoted and used Nehemiah's private diary in much the same way as the Book of Ezra includes full quotations from official documents, etc. The genealogy in 12:11 and 22 includes details which probably were added considerably later but these only related to one or two names.

MEMORIZE THE FOLLOWING DETAILS

KEY WORDS – Restoration or Reformation Pray – Watch – Work

KEY VERSES – 1:4; 2:4 & 18; 4:6 & 9

NUMBER OF CHAPTERS – 13

The principal message of the book is particularly applicable to Christian workers emphasizing as it does the place of prayer and perseverance in the work of God. A later paragraph will deal with Nehemiah and from his life and work these points will be reemphasized.

L.A.T. VAN DOOREN

The following is an Analysis of the Book:

The Wall Rebuilt	1:1 - 7:3
The People Re-consecrated	7:4 - 10:39
The Walls Dedicated	11: 1 - 12:47
The People Corrected	13: 1-31

There are several outstanding chapters – that is why the book should be reread as often as possible. Pay special attention to Nehemiah's diary – chs. 1-7. Also observe the stand he takes against the enemies of the people of God. Further portions that repay rereading are to be found in chapter 8:1-12 dealing with the reading of the law and the prayer of the Levites in chapter 9:4-38. Also particularly observe Nehemiah's energetic dealings with evil-doers and wrong practices – 13:1-31.

Nehemiah is an outstanding man of God who occupied a position of responsibility and of prominence in the Imperial Court at Shushan. He had the prospect of a secure future, ease and luxury for his position would be one of the highest and most trusted in the Persian court. Nehemiah reveals himself as a Man of Concern for the well-being of the people and the purposes of God and as a man of Prayer and Action who exchanges position, ease and comfort, wealth and luxury for work, danger and hardship in the service of the Lord. By his business-like application to the work of God he reveals also statesman-like abilities coupled with perseverance. He remains undisturbed and undismayed even when confronted by overwhelming opposition from without and opposition and murmurings from within. He recognizes that the work in which he is engaged for God is of greater importance than all else – see 6:3.

There are repeated references to prayer. Indeed the book begins and ends with prayer. Observe the following:

1:5-11; 2:4; 4:4 & 9; 5:19; 6:9 & 14; 13:14,22,29,31

Take particular note of the closing phrase of 8:10.

THE BEST OF CAPERNWRAY

Throughout the Book there is a constant emphasis on the place of prayer, watchfulness and work and in chapter 3 it will be observed that each party commences to work nearest their own home. This is in accordance with God's program for His people today, even as when He said to His disciples prior to His ascension – Acts 1:8 – 'Beginning at Jerusalem'!

ESTHER

'Operation 39' – Lesson 17

The Book of Esther is second to none as a literary gem – full of swift-moving drama, plot and counterplot. Read the whole of the Book through. You want to do so more than once. Psalm 11 and Isaiah 54:17 form an apt commentary on this writing.

The Book is called Esther after the name of one of the chief characters. It is the second book in the Bible to be named after a woman and in the Hebrew Bible is found in the section known as the Hagiographa or Psalms and was one of the five rolls. It was read annually in the Synagogues at the Feast of Purim. This Feast was instituted to commemorate the deliverance of the Jews recorded in the closing section of the Book.

The events recorded took place within the gap between chapters 6 and 7 of the Book of Ezra referred to in Lesson 15. It is usually dated as taking place between 484 and 465 B.C.

Note of the time references in the Book: 1:3; 2:12 and 16; 3:7. The Ahasuerus mentioned in the book was the Xerxes who, when he came to Greece by land, lost the Battle of Thermopylae and later lost to the Greeks by sea at Salamis – 480 B.C. It is thought that the great feast referred to in chapter 1 was held prior to the expedition and to celebrate the going forth against Greece. If this is so, there are four years during which this Campaign took place between the events recorded in ch. 1:3-4 and ch. 2:12-16.

The name of the writer cannot be stated with certainty. According to Jewish tradition it is ascribed to Ezra or Mordecai. Quite possibly Ezra the Scribe was responsible for its final compilation and it is thought to have been copied to a considerable extent from Persian official state records. This would account for the detailed references to names of servants – 1:10; Provincial rulers – 1:14; intimate details such as colors, draperies, furnishings – 1:6, etc. There are other references to Persian etiquette and customs, and descriptive references such as Mordecai the Jew and Esther the Queen. There are 187 references to the name of the Persian King. These details do not however in any way affect the inspiration of the book for it was by God's overruling that such selections were made, whether the human writer was Mordecai, Ezra or Scribes of the Great Synagogue.

MEMORIZE THE FOLLOWING DETAILS

KEY WORD – Providence

KEY VERSE – 4:14

NUMBER OF CHAPTERS – 10

One particular and outstanding feature of the Book is that there is no direct reference to the name of God or the Lord. This is in contrast to the 187 references to the name of the Persian king. For this reason there are those who stated it should not have a place in Holy Scripture. Furthermore it is never quoted in the New Testament and makes no reference to prayer or the observance of the Jewish law.

It was however regarded in olden time by the Jews as being particularly sacred. The Rabbis quoted Deuteronomy 31:18 as a reason why God's name was not mentioned, namely, that God had hidden His face from His people because of their sin.

It has however been pointed out in more recent times that the name of God appears in acrostic form; in two instances, as initial letters and in two instances as final letters. It is of course only possible to discern this in the original Hebrew. The references however are 1:20; 5:4; 5:13 and 7:7.

The fact remains that even if God is not referred to directly, yet He is to be seen at work in the background bringing deliverance to His people.

"Behind the dim unknown standeth God within the shadow keeping watch above His own"

A short Book such as that of Esther with its gripping story lends itself to several methods of Analysis. The Following are suggested:

I. The Jews in Great Danger – chs. 1 – 4

II. The Jews Experience Great Deliverance – chs. 5 – 10

The Feast of Ahasuerus	1 – 2
The Feasts of Esther	3 – 7
The Feast of Purim	8 - 10

Particularly observe ch. 4:14 and the closing phrase of 4:16 and compare Romans 12:1-2.

It has been pointed out previously that this Book reveals the providential workings of God on behalf of His people even when they have not remained true to Him for the Jews in Persia should have returned to the Promised Land. But the Lord abides faithful and although His name is concealed His hand is seen to be at work. Compare Psalm 121:3-5; Isaiah 63:9; Psalm 48:14; Hebrews 13:5-6.

"He abideth faithful, He cannot deny Himself"

Questions on the Book of Esther

1. Quote a verse from Isaiah which forms an apt commentary on the Book of Esther.
2. At which Feast of the Jews was the Book of Esther read annually?
3. When did the events recorded in Esther take place?
   What do you know concerning the authorship of this Book?
4. State the following details: Key Word, Key Verse and No. of Chapters.
5. Give two peculiar features of this book.
6. Give one or two short analyses of the book.

JOB

'Operation 39' – Lesson 18

When did you last read this book right through? As you turn to the study of it, read the book following the suggestions given in the following notes so as to read the sequence of Job's speeches and replies given by his friends without interruption. Turn also to Romans 8:28 and to John 16:20 & 33.

It is called The Book of Job because the story centers around Job as the man of God who is the chief character in the narrative. In the Hebrew Bible it is found within the Hagiographa.

It is impossible to date the story of Job. It is however generally considered to have been one of the earliest, if not the earliest, of the Old Testament writings. This would date the narrative as having taken place in the Patriarchal times and would seem to be in accordance with the age to which Job lived – 42:16. There is no reference by Job's friends to the miracles preceding and attending the story of the Exodus and this also suggests that the events took place prior to the story of the Exodus. Furthermore, Job is seen acting as High Priest in his family and this was not allowed after the exodus and the appointment of Aaron. Eliphaz was a descendant of Esau for he is referred to in chapter 4, verse 1 as Eliphaz the Temanite and Teman was the son of Eliphaz who was the son of Esau – Genesis 36:10-11.

Job (likewise Melchisedec of whom we read in Genesis) is therefore a character of whom we know little but who was a worshipper of God. There is no doubt whatsoever that he was a living character and not a fictitious figure for he is referred to in Ezekiel 14:14 and 20; James 5:11. He is said to have dwelt at Uz which is also referred to in Lamentations 4:21 as being in Edom. He was evidently a man of great wealth occupying a high and respected position and was one of the greatest men of the East in his day. Coupled with these facts which emerge from the book, he is known to be a man of perfect integrity and upright life whose character was further refined by the suffering which he endured.

The author is unknown. There are those who think it could have been Elihu referred to in chapter 32 but it is best to recognize the fact that there is no conclusive evidence as to who the author was. The book deals with the great problem of all ages, the problem of suffering. The final answer to that problem is not given in this writing nor does Job find his questions answered but he is however brought to the position where he lays aside his questions and trusts implicitly in the Lord, thus in true and full submission he finds comfort and restoration, reward and increased blessing.

MEMORIZE THE FOLLOWING DETAILS

KEY WORD – Trial

THEME – Tested but Triumphant

KEY VERSE – 1:9

NUMBER OF CHAPTERS – 42

OUTSTANDING CHAPTER - 38

The story of Job's calamities and the visit of his friends is told in dramatic form. For this reason the book is quite distinctive from every other book of the Old Testament. The literary from and style stamp it as being one of the greatest writings in the Bible and indeed in the world. It will be helpful both to read the Book and to study it according to the series of speeches.

The following is a brief Analysis of the Book:

THE BEST OF CAPERNWRAY

Job and Satan	1 - 2
Job and his Friends	3 - 31
Job and Elihu	32 - 37
Job and God	38 - 42

The following further Analysis will assist in a further study of the Book:

I. Job and Satan – chs. 1 – 2

- Job – his purity, prosperity and piety
- Satan – his restlessness allowed to accuse Job before God: revealed as having considerable power but limited and under the jurisdiction of God.

II. Job and his Friends – chs. 3 – 31

It will be observed that Job's speeches may be divided into three groups, likewise the replies of his friends:

- Job's first series of Three Speeches – found in chs. 3, 6, 7, 9 and 10. The key thought in these speeches may be summed up in one word – 'Perplexity'

Read the following verses found within these speeches: 3:20; 7:21 and 10:2

- The Answers of Job's friends: Eliphaz – chs. 4 & 5 : Bildad – ch. 8 : Zophar – ch. 11
- Job's second series of Three Speeches – found in chapters 12, 13, 14, 16, 17 and 19.
- The key thought of these speeches can be summed up in the word 'Trust.'

Read the following found within these speeches: 13:15; 14:14; 16:19; 19:25-26.

- The answers of Job's friends: Eliphaz – ch. 15 : Bildad – ch. 18 : Zophar – ch. 20.

- Job's third series of Three Speeches – chs. 21, 23, 24 and 26-31. The key thought of these three speeches may be summed up in the phrase 'God Knows.'

Read the following verses found within the speeches – 21:7 & 22; 24:1; 28:12 & 23.

- The answers of Job's Friends: Eliphaz – ch. 22: Bildad – ch. 25 : Zophar – no further answer.

III. Job and Elihu – ch. 32 – 37

- Elihu attributes Job's trouble to his self-righteousness and God's Sovereignty and comes nearer the truth than the other three friends, calling upon Job to consider the wondrous works of God.

Read the following Scriptures: 32:3; 33:30.

IV. Job and God – ch. 38 – 42

- God's Reproof and Revelation – ch. 38-39; 40-41. In particular read 38:1-41

- Job's Repentance and Restoration. In particular read 40:3-5; 42:1-17.

In the above outline there is reference to the replies made by Job's three friends, Eliphaz, Bildad and Zophar.

The speeches of Eliphaz are uttered with <u>Sympathy</u> – for instance see such verses as 4:3-5; 15:20-21; 22:21.

The speeches of Bildad are uttered with <u>Severity</u> – for instance see such verses as 8:6; 18:5; 25:6.

The speeches of Zophar are uttered with <u>Bigotry</u> – see such verses as 11:3; 20:26.

Job's friends bring him no real comfort nor do they utter that which is the truth concerning Job, God and suffering and to a large extent portray ignorance of the vital issues at stake. In truth, they can hardly be called comforters or friends! Hence, the phrase 'Job's Comforters!'

While this Book does not contain the full answer to the question or to the problem of suffering yet in the opening two chapters God does, as it were, draw aside the veil and reveal deeper issues. It is clear that personal suffering is not to be thought of as being a direct result of personal sin, as was the case so often in times past. It reveals that suffering and pain is not always sent as chastisement but it can also have its purpose in testing and revealing character. Indeed, it is by suffering that character is so often refined and stabilized and it promotes greater dependence upon God and submission to His ways.

The attitude of Job's friends and others in times past can be aptly summed up in the question 'How can this man be godly if he suffers?' In reply to this question the further question may be asked 'How can this man be God-like if he knows nothing of suffering?' In this connection turn to Hebrews 2:10, where it is stated that suffering added to the experience of Christ that which was only possible through suffering.

The whole story of the Book is a commentary on the history of man from creation to completed redemption. Observe the following movements in the Book:

- Man – fallen and tried
- Sinning and suffering
- Human help offered in the way of legality, morality and philosophy
- The need of and the revelation of God
- Humbled, repentant and believing
- Restoration to an infinitely better state than previously

Your attention has already been directed to chapter 38 as being a Scripture of outstanding importance and containing sublime truth. In addition, particularly observe the following verses: 9:2; 9:32-33; 13:15; 14:1-2; 19:23-26; 42:3; 28:28.

After reading The Book of Job, every child of God should be warned not to be unduly hasty or critical in their judgment of another believer for God alone knows the full story behind many outward events in this life.

To yield without question to the Lord and to draw near to Him in complete dependence and full submission to enter into ultimate blessing and the true fulfillment of God's purposes for the individual life.

PSALMS

'Operation 39' – Lesson 19

Unlike the majority of the books in the Bible, The Book of Psalms is not one that you should necessarily try to read through at one sitting. It is the Hymn Book of the Hebrews and as our present-day hymn books reflect the many varied experiences of the soul so the Psalms were written out of a variety of experiences and each Psalm should be read as a hymn which is complete in itself. You will find it helpful if with your notebook at your side you seek to sum up the main message or content of each Psalm under one short phrase or title, as for main message or content of each Psalm under one short phrase or title, as for instance, Psalm 1: The contrast between the Godly and the Ungodly; Psalm 2: The Lord my King; Psalm 3: The Lord my Shield; Psalm 23: The Lord my Shepherd.

The Book of Psalms is known as the Psalter and is divided into five sections or books. The five sections or books are as follows:

Book 1	1 - 41	Book 4	90 - 106
Book 2	42 - 72	Book 5	107-150
Book 3	73 - 89		

Each of these sections ends with a note of praise ascribing glory to God. Make a special note of the following Scriptures in your Bible: 41:13; 72:19-20; 89:52; 106:48; 150:5.

You may well raise the question as to why the Psalter has been divided into five sections for the books are not arranged according to their chronological order. There is however discernable a similarity of subject matter within the five sections although this statement must only be accepted in a very general sense and is by no means arbitrary.

Ancient Hebrew tradition tells us that Moses gave to the Children of Israel the Five Books of the Law and likewise David gave them the five books of the Psalms. A careful study does reveal a certain similarity between the five books of the Pentateuch and the five books of the Psalms. While David is often thought of as the author of the Psalms, it must be remembered that while he wrote many of the Psalms there were many other authors as well. It is because he is the principal author that the book is sometimes known as David's Psalter or The Treasury of David.

There are 150 Psalms and of these the authors are indicated by the titles appearing at the head of the Psalms. 73 Psalms are attributed to David; 2 to Solomon; 1 to Moses; 10 to Hezekiah (Psalms 120-139 – Isaiah 38:20); 10 to the School of Korah; 12 to the School of Asaph; 1 to Ethan (Psalm 89); 1 to Heman (Psalm 138). It is thought that Jeremiah may have been the author of Psalm 137, Haggai of Psalm 146 and Zechariah the author of Psalm 137. This is on the authority of the Septuagint. It is also thought that Ezra may have written Psalm 119. The remainder of the Psalms are anonymous.

It has already been stated above that the Psalms are not arranged in chronological order and it is not possible to fix the dates of the individual writings. Of those written by David, a number are stated to be related to certain events in his career but even these subtitles cannot necessarily be considered authoritative although they may be helpful. They are not of course part of the inspired text.

The great period of song in Israel's history began with David, the sweet singer of Israel and extended to the time of Hezekiah. No doubt the majority of the Psalms belong to this period. The songs of degrees or pilgrim Psalms are thought to have been these which were sung by the returning exiles after the Babylonian captivity. Some may have been composed at that date.

THE BEST OF CAPERNWRAY

It is impossible to pick out, as in the case of most of the other books of the Old Testament, the key word or verse as the Psalms survey the whole realm of human experience in relation to God. You will however find it helpful and desirable to memorize the number and words of certain outstanding Psalms, for instance:

Psalm 1 – with its contrasting pictures of the godly and the ungodly

The Shepherd Psalm – 23

David's penitential Psalm – 51

The Covenant Psalm – 121

Psalm of sowing and reaping – 126

Psalm of Joy – 100

Bless the Lord Psalm – 103

The Call to Praise the Lord – 150

It would be possible to pick out many other Psalms. You are asked to choose at least one Psalm and learn it by heart.

Reference has been made to similarity between the Five Books of Moses and the Five Books of the Psalms. Again let it be stated that this should be considered only in a very general and not in an arbitrary sense, but the correspondence is set out below:

Genesis	Psalms 1 – 41	Speaks of man's true blessedness, his fall and recovery. In this section in Psalms 8 and 19 there are references to creation and the flood.
Exodus	Psalms 42 - 72	Israel's ruin is referred to in Psalms 42-49. Psalms 50-72 emphasize the Redeemer and the redemption that belongs to the people of God. In Psalms 66 and 68 there are references to the crossing of the Red Sea.

Leviticus	Psalms 73 – 89	These Psalms deal mainly with the praise and worship of God especially Psalms 74 and 84.
Numbers	Psalms 90 – 106	Psalm 90 was written during the wanderings in the wilderness by Moses. There are references to the blessing of the earth which was both needed and anticipated. Psalms 95 and 100 refer to the wilderness wanderings.
Deuteronomy	Psalms 107 – 150	Here there is emphasis on the Word of God, even as in Deuteronomy there is the repetition of the Law. In particular note Psalm 119.

A further method of analysis reveals that each of the books emphasizes a different revelation of God:

Psalms 1 – 41	Present the Lord as Savior – Key Verse 23:1
Psalms 42 – 72	Present the Lord as King – Key Verse 45:6
Psalms 73 – 89	Present the Lord as the Guide and Answer for every need – Key Verse 86:7
Psalms 90 – 106	Present the Lord as the Eternal One – Key Verse 102:27
Psalms 107 – 150	Present the Lord as the One who does all things well – Key Verse 107:8

Certain Psalms which speak of the Lord the Messiah are known as Messianic Psalms. They are 16, 22, 24, 40, 68, 69 and 118.

Psalm 119 speaks in every verse of the Word of God under such titles as 'Thy Word,' 'The Law of the Lord,' 'Testimonies,' 'Precepts,' 'Statutes,' etc. It is divided into 22 sections corresponding to the 22 letters in the Hebrew alphabet. Each verse in the respective sections commence with same initial letter to be found at the head of the section. This no doubt was designed to assist in memorization of the Psalm.

It was Charles Haddon Spurgeon who said of this book 'The Book of Psalms instructs us in the use of wings as well as words. It sets us both mounting and singing.' This is the book to which every believer may turn no matter what the immediate need may be, whether it be a time of grief or sorrow; of fear or doubt. Whether the human heart is oppressed with the cares or anxieties or whether it is a time of special joy, gladness and thanksgiving. Here as nowhere else will be found that which gives expression to the deepest thoughts and indeed the secret joys and sorrows of the heart of the child of God. Hence it is the outstanding devotional book of the Bible. It has been said that elsewhere in the Scriptures God is speaking to man but in the book of Psalms man is represented as speaking to God.

Evidence of the appeal that the Book of Psalms makes is shown by the fact that out of 300 or so direct references from the Old Testament which are to be found in the New, it is said that 116 are from the Psalms. It will be remembered that on the Day of Pentecost Peter quoted from the Psalms as he spoke of the resurrection of the Lord Jesus.

Conclude your study of this book by carrying out the exhortation of Psalm 29, verse 2.

QUESTIONS ON THE BOOK OF PSALMS

1. How many songs are there in the Book of Psalms?

2. State the divisions into which the Psalter is usually divided, giving the actual references of the Psalms.

3. State how each of these sections end.

4. How many Psalms are said to have been written by David? How many by Solomon and how many by Moses?

5. Set out a similarity between the divisions of the Book of Psalms and the Pentateuch.

6. What is your favorite Psalm? Give your reasons for choosing this particular one.

7. Have you any comment to make with regard to the quotations from the Book of Psalms which is to be found in the New Testament?

PROVERBS

'Operation 39' – Lesson 20

As the Book of Psalms is different from all others in the Bible so for another reason the Book of Proverbs is distinctive from the remainder of Scripture. It will at once be seen that it is a collection of pithy sayings, hence the name 'Proverbs.' The reading through of this Book presents its difficulties for each Proverb is complete in itself and says so much in so few words! Nevertheless, to read the Book through carefully and thoughtfully will bring its own rich reward and have an impact on your life.

To teach by proverbs is one of the most ancient forms of instruction; probably the most ancient. Every nation would appear to have its proverbs and this is particularly true of the East. Indeed, the East seems to have been the original home of Proverbs and many of the proverbs in our own tongue have their origin in the East. To teach by proverbs was a method well suited to the ancient times when there were few books and few who could read or write. Therefore truth and practical advice could be more easily remembered when couched in clear crisp sentences. In the day in which we live when of books there is no end, people are not inclined to memorize so much. Nevertheless, the proverb still holds a foremost place in our language.

It must be remembered that the Book of Proverbs is not purely human wisdom. These proverbs have been written and selected by Divine inspiration and are intended to be of practical help in our daily life. It is true that in the Book of Proverbs the problems of life are surveyed in the main from the human point of view but God has placed them on record for our admonition and instruction in righteousness. As you read the book you will perceive it is full of practical godliness and sanctified common sense.

The Proverbs can be attributed to a number of human authors. In 1 Kings 4:32 it is stated 'Solomon spoke 3,000 Proverbs.' In Ecclesiastes 12:9 it is state 'Solomon sought out and set in order many proverbs.' Many no doubt, of these proverbs are contained within the Book that you are now studying. There is also reference to certain of the proverbs being the words of the wise and it is thought that these were Solomon's teachers. In addition, is reference to the words of Agur and Lamuel. There is also a reference to a further selection of the Proverbs of Solomon by the men of Hezekiah – 25:1. These details may be summarized as follows:

Introduction	1:1-5
The Words of the Wise	1:6 – 9:18
The Proverbs of the Words of the Wise	19:20 – 24:34
The Proverbs of Solomon	25:1 – 29:27
Proverbs of Agur	30:1-33
The Proverbs of Lemuel – taught him by his mother	31:1-31

The book cannot be analyzed in the usual way and the best method of studying Proverbs is to take a concordance and trace through the 31 chapters all that is said on various subjects. This at once opens up a tremendous field of study on a variety of different subjects ranging from the wise man to the fool; from wisdom to folly; from riches to poverty; from diligence to idleness; from justice to dishonesty; from goodness to gluttony; from virtue to vice, gluttony, strife and revenge.

It will be observed that there are several different forms in which the Proverbs are couched. For instance, by way of <u>Contrast</u>, as 1:7. <u>Repetition</u> is used – 1:8; a third form is by way of <u>Comparison</u> – 17:10. There are certain <u>Sequences</u>, as for instance on fools – 26:3-12.

It is difficult to select a Key Verse or Word as in the case of most of the other books of the Bible but you should memorize the following two verses which give an apt summary of the message of the book – 9:10 and 15:33. Number of chapters – 31.

Two outstanding passages which personify Wisdom are 1:20-33 and 8:1 - 9, 12.

Observe the Lord's promise on the subjects of guidance in 3:5-6; and Liberty in 11:24-25.

The following are passages which you should learn by heart:

3:5-9, particularly verses 5 and 6; 6:6-11; 11:30; 11:24-25. Compare 2 Corinthians 9:6-8

Read 1: 5. The test of wisdom is that you hear and thereby profit and so increase in learning. To hear in the truest sense of the word is to allow that which you hear to become a part of your very life. Therefore, to hear the Word of God as contained in the Proverbs leads to a close and humble walk with the Lord which is true wisdom and the beginning of godliness.

QUESTIONS ON THE BOOK OF PROVERBS

1. State briefly the advantages of teaching by form of proverbial sayings or proverbs.
2. Who was the most prolific speaker and writer of Proverbs?
3. Give one of the most profitable ways of studying the book of Proverbs.
4. State the several different forms in which the Proverbs are couched.
5. State which passage in the book of Proverbs you have learned by heart.
6. Give two outstanding verses which contain the promise of the Lord's guidance to His own.
7. Do you remember the promise of 8:17?
8. Do you remember what is said of a good name in chapter 22?

ECCLESIASTES

'Operation 39' – Lesson 21

Please read the Book through. It is relatively short and there should be little difficulty in reading it without interruption.

In addition to the title 'Ecclesiastes' the book has the alternative title of 'The Preacher.' This is derived from the Septuagint and is intended to be a translation of the Hebrew title 'Koheleth' which signifies a person who convenes and addresses an assembly.

It is found in the Hagiographa, that is, it forms part of the Wisdom literature of the Old Testament.

Although its authorship has been doubted by some it is generally accepted as having been written by Solomon and there is no reason why this should not be accepted as a fact – 1:1. Indeed it would appear in some measure to be a brief autobiography of Solomon's life, of how he sought happiness after he ceased to walk in the ways of his father, David, and fell away from his early faith and reliance upon God. The Book has been called the saddest book in the Bible and this statement has added emphasis if it is considered as revealing the unhappy state of Solomon's heart resulting in complete dissatisfaction despite his outstanding achievements and his undoubted intellectual ability. It contains the record of man's futile ramblings leading to frustration and disappointment when God is left out of the life.

In view of the concluding two verses – 12:13-14 – the question might well be asked as to whether Solomon returned at the end of his days to a God-fearing manner of life.

L.A.T. VAN DOOREN

The references to The Preacher are 1:1; 2:12; 7:7; 12:8-10.

MEMORIZE THE FOLLOWING DETAILS

KEY WORD – Vanity

KEY PHRASE – Under the sun

NUMBER OF CHAPERS – 12

There are those who would question whether the Book of Ecclesiastes should be included in the Canon of Scripture. Indeed, there have been those who have appealed to its content in support of a skeptical philosophy of life. There are certain statements which seem to be at first glance contradictory to general Bible teaching and to a code of conduct which is contrary to that which should be expected from the true Christian. It is necessary however to understand the purpose for which the Book is written for an explanation of such details.

As you read the Book you will realize that it makes clear that life apart from God is full of disappointment, weariness, frustration and without any true purpose. It is written from the point of view of the natural man as is indicated by the key phrase 'under the sun,' and similar phrases. It reveals the experiment of trying to live without God and although there may be attainment in the intellectual and material realms, yet this leads only to bitterness in view of the fact that there is no lasting or true satisfaction to be found in these attainments. The Book is therefore an important one in making clear the futility, disappointment, sorrow and sadness of the life that is lived without God. Indeed, such a manner of life is 'vanity of vanities.'

Compare the following passages with the New Testament references and it will be seen that there are quotations or allusions to this Book in the New Testament:

5:1 with 1 Timothy 3:15	7:2 with Matthew 5:3-4
5:2 with Matthew 6:7	11:5 with John 3:8
5:6 with I Corinthians 11:10	12:14 with 2 Corinthians 5:10
6:2 with Luke 12:20	

Passages which appear to be opposites to much of the general teaching of the Word of God and of Christian conduct are as follows. We must however bear in mind the statement made above in the paragraph beginning "There are those who would question…"

1:15; 2:24; 3:3,4,8,11,19,20; 7:16-17; 8:15

As has been stated above, the key phrase is 'Under the sun.' This occurs 29 times. Other words or phrases occurring with frequency are

Vanity – 37 times; Under the Heaven – 3; Under the Earth – 7

These words and phrases indicate the point of view from which the Book is written. It gives a dismal story of man living under the sun and without God. Indeed the references to God are impersonal, such as, the Creator of man – 12:1. There is no use of the title Jehovah or Lord in the Book. The Book does not contain the significant phrase used by prophets; namely, 'Thus saith the Lord.' As stated above, its value is in serving to emphasize the futility of life apart from God.

The following is a brief Analysis:

I. The Problem stated – 1:1-3

II. The Search for Satisfaction – 1:4 – 12:12

The Preacher searches for satisfaction in the following ways:

- In Nature
- In Wisdom and Philosophy
- In Pleasure
- In Building, Possessions and Culture
- In Materialism
- In Fatalism
- In Varied Aspects of Life
- In Formal Religion

- In Wealth
- In Morality

III. The End of the Search – 12:13-14

While it is true this Book contains the story of a man's disillusionment, it must be remembered that it was written down under the direction of the Holy Spirit of God, otherwise the writing would not be worthy of a place in the Canon of Scripture. It has been pointed out that the language used is consistent with discoveries concerning evaporation and storm currents – see 1:6-7. Furthermore in chapter 12 there is a poetical description of growing old and finally of death itself. 12:1-7 should be reread with this in mind and 12:1 memorized.

The Book of Ecclesiastes might be a wearisome book if there was no Gospel of the Grace of God which reveals the way of true satisfaction, happiness and peace with God. It is only as God's way of Salvation is accepted that there is discovered a true purpose in life. 'If the Son shall make you free, ye shall be free indeed' and in true submission to the claims of Christ there is found to be a purpose and a good and acceptable and perfect will of God for every individual. In contrast to the key phrase 'under the sun' there is the glorious truth stated in Ephesians that the believer is identified and one with Christ in the place of heavenly triumph 'in heavenly places.' In Christ there is to be found a life that is satisfying and enables the believer to live in the world and yet to be triumphant and victorious.

Contrast the statement made in 1:15 with the answer to be found in Isaiah 40:4 and 42:16; Luke 3:5 and 13:13. Also compare Philippians 2:15.

Contrast 1:9 with 2 Corinthians 5:17 and Revelation 21:5.

You are not called to live under the circumstances but to be triumphant in Christ in and through the changing pattern of life here below.

THE BEST OF CAPERNWRAY

QUESTIONS ON THE BOOK OF ECCLESIASTES

1. Give the alternative titles to the Book of Ecclesiastes.

2. Where is this to be found in the Hebrew Bible?

3. Give the Key Word, Key Phrase and number of chapters found in the book.

4. State briefly one or two reasons why this Book has a place in the Canon of Scripture.

5. In addition to the key phrase given in answer to question 3 above give other words or phrases which are found frequently.

6. Write out in full from memory 12:1.

7. Who is the author and what is the Book thought to be as far as he personally is concerned?

8. Give a brief Analysis of the book.

9. Is there any answer to be found to the phrase 'under the sun' in the New Testament?

SONG OF SOLOMON

'Operation 39' – Lesson 22

Time should be taken to read the eight chapters of this Book through carefully, quietly and prayerfully. It is not a Book that can be read hurriedly if one is to derive spiritual profit from the reading. It is also called 'Canticles.'

It is essential to remember that the original writing is in the form of poetry and as such the language is poetical. It will be helpful to remember that it is also written in the figurative language of the Orientals so that expressions that Westerners would hesitate to use are found in this Book, and these would not be out of place in an Eastern love song.

In the Hebrew Bible, the Song of Solomon is found in the Hagiographa and is one of the Five Rolls. It was and still is regularly sung during the Passover Feast. This in itself seems to denote something of its typical significance and therefore it may be assumed that the truth found in this book can only be truly appreciated and understood by those who have accepted the Lord Jesus as their own Passover Lamb and now know Him as the Lover of their soul.

The Jews have always held this writing in the highest esteem. For instance, they compared The Book of Proverbs to the Outer Court of the Temple, Ecclesiastes to the Holy Place and the Song of Solomon to the Holiest of all. This again indicated something of the nature of the contents of the Book for it is descriptive of the blessed union and intimate fellowship between the Lord and the believer.

In chapter 1, verse 1 it is described as being the Song of Songs which is Solomon's. In 1 Kings 4:32 it is said that Solomon's Songs numbered 1,005. This is his Song of Songs! Truly there is no song to be compared to that of the Song of love and particularly between the Lord Jesus, who loved and gave Himself for the church and for the individual believer. There is no reason whatsoever to doubt the fact that Solomon was the author.

It is difficult to Analyze or set out other details of this writing as can so often be done in the case of the other Books of the Bible. Nevertheless, think over the following and memorize:

KEY WORD – Love

KEY VERSE – 8:6-7

THEME – Communion between Christ and the Child of God

NUMBER OF CHAPTERS – 8

There are several possible interpretations to this book. There are those who believe that the writing is based on an actual love story and this no doubt is so. It was been suggested that the story of love portrayed here is that between Solomon and Pharoah's daughter. See 1 Kings 3:1; 7:8; 9:24; and Song of Solomon 1:9; 6:12.

It has also been suggested that it is an account of how Solomon wooed and won the Shunamite lass. Shunem was on the southwest slopes of Little Hermon, now situated in the country of Lebanon. There are others who see in the story an account of the love between a shepherd and a maiden and an attempt by Solomon to turn the heart of the maiden to himself but who did nevertheless stand true to her first shepherd lover.

Is it possible to decide which is the correct view? Whatever your answer may be to that question it is more important to discover the truth that God has set forth in this particular portion of His Word and in the doing so come closer in fellowship and communion with Christ Himself.

The methods of interpretation of the Book vary considerably. There are those who say it is historical, that is depicting in poetical form the history of the Jews from Abraham to the coming of their Messiah or the deliverance of the people of God from Egypt followed by wanderings in the Wilderness and finally their entrance into Canaan. No doubt there are lessons such as this to be found in the story, for waywardness and restoration and the constant wooing of the lover is all depicted here.

For the present day believer, the story would seem To be an allegory depicting the union of Christ and of the church or to make a more personal application the story depicts the Love of the Lord and His wooing and winning of a soul resulting in indescribable bliss and fellowship. This is why it is the Song of Songs! Without doubt all of the above suggestions have their place in interpreting this writing. It is significant to discover that many of God's choicest saints have declared that this book has been of the greatest help to them and a source of constant blessing to their soul.

It is not easy to discern the person or persons speaking for 'the whispers of love' and conversation goes backwards and forwards interspersed here and there by the daughters of Jerusalem – 2:7; 3:5; 5:8-9.

It has already been stated above that the Book almost defied analysis and differing interpretations will suggest a different form of analysis.

The following is a suggestion:

The Lovers' Delight in each other	1:1 – 2:7
The Deepening Love	2:8 – 3:5
The Joy and Delights of the Marriage	3:6 – 5:1
The Happy Reunion following Sleep and Absence	5:2 – 8:4
The True nature of Love	8:5 – 14

The Song of Songs is better read on the knees than studied at a desk! No doubt the Spirit of God will lift out certain verses and bring them home to your mind and conscience as you quietly read it through. For instance, many a Christian worker has been challenged by the latter part of 1:6. How easy it is to be engaged in Christian service and be neglectful of your own vineyard, that is, vital communion with the Lord and your own personal Christian life.

Who cannot rejoice in the truth of 2:4?

Who cannot take the warning of 2:14? Be ready for such whispers of love from the Spirit of the Lord during your reading and meditation of this writing.

It should not be overlooked that while it would seem that God desires to lead us into closer fellowship with Himself and this no doubt is the main purpose of the writing yet it serves to emphasize the sanctity of human love and the marriage vow.

ISAIAH

'Operation 39' – Lesson 23

It would be a difficult task to sit down and read this Book without break or interruption and therefore it is suggested that it should be read in stages according to the outline given below. It is important to know if possible something of the historic background of the prophets and you are therefore referred to the following references in the historic books in the Old Testament which approximately cover the period during which Isaiah ministered. It would be helpful to read these portions – 2 Kings 15:1 – 20:1; 2 Chronicles 26:1 – 33:1; they cover a period of about 60 years from 760 B.C.

Isaiah received his commission from the Lord in the closing years of the reign of King Uzziah and was evidently still a very young prophet when he had his vision in the year that King Uzziah died – chapter 6. He continued his prophetic ministry during the reigns of Jothan and Ahaz and Hezekiah and it is thought that he died as a martyr in the reign of the wicked king Manasseh. His period of ministry must have been of very long duration and tradition says that he was put to death at the age of 120. He is said to have suffered a very violent form of death such as is described in Hebrews 11:37 'being sawn asunder.'

Isaiah was a prophet to Judah; i.e., the Southern Kingdom, and a man of outstanding influence and ability. He was the son of Amoz who is thought to have been a younger son of Joash, King of Judah. This would mean that Isaiah was of royal blood. His wife's name was Huldah, who also shared the prophetic gifts and is one of the three women numbered among the prophets. He had sons and their names have prophetic significance. Indeed we read in chapter 8, verse 8 that both he and his children had been given by the Lord for signs and wonders in Israel. One son is named Shaarjashub, meaning 'the remnant shall return.' His name sums up to some extent the message of chapters 40 – 66. Another son was named Maher-shalal-hash-baz, meaning 'make haste' or 'speed to the spoil,' 'hasten or hurry to the prey.' This to some extent represents the content of chapters 1 – 39. The name Isaiah means 'Salvation of the Lord,' or 'Jehovah is Salvation' and this sums up the message of the whole book. It was not infrequent that God, through the prophets, applied and illustrated their message from their family life. In other words the man and his message were complementary the one to the other.

Although Isaiah was a prophet it will be seen that he also became a statesman in his advice to the kings and was undoubtedly a man of outstanding ability and intellectual attainment. This is revealed by the writing which is one of the finest of the prophetic writings of the Old Testament. It is written in rich and noble language and with a simplicity and clarity of meaning. All but four chapters; namely 36-39 inclusive, are written in poetry. The four chapters referred to are prose. You would find it helpful to read this and indeed other of the books of the prophets in the revised version of 1885 as this preserves the poetic form more than the Authorized Version.

It was not until a little over a century ago that doubts were raised as to whether Isaiah was the author of the whole of this book or not and since then much discussion has raged around the question of Isaiah's authorship as there are those who speak of the second Isaiah, the Babylonian Isaiah and so forth. The main objection to Isaiah being the author of the latter part of the book; namely, from chapter 40 onwards, seems to be because this concerns itself to a great extent with predictions which were still future to Isaiah's day and rather than accept the fact that God, by His Holy Spirit was able to make known the events to His prophet the theories were put forward that the latter section of the book was written by a later prophet. This criticism does however spring out of unbelief and an attitude that refuses to recognize God's part in directing the prophecy and may be dismissed as the work of those who seek to undermine and destroy the authority of God's Word.

The Jews always accepted the Book as a whole and have never cast any doubt upon the authorship of Isaiah. Furthermore in the New Testament there are 21 references to Isaiah being the writer of this book. Ten of these quotations are taken from chapters 1 – 39 and eleven quotations are taken from chapters 40 – 66. This in itself must be accepted as quite conclusive, if we accept the Word of God for what it claims to be; namely, THE WORD OF GOD.

A careful study of the Book will however reveal that there is an intimate connection between the earlier chapters where prophecies are referred to as being fulfilled and in the later chapters Isaiah leads his reader to believe that as prophecy has been fulfilled in the past so predictions concerning the future will likewise be fulfilled. For instance see 48:3-5. Furthermore there is a similarity of language and style manifest throughout the whole book testifying to the unity of the whole.

MEMORIZE THE FOLLOWING DETAILS

KEY WORD – Salvation

KEY PHRASES AND THEME – The Holy One of Israel and Salvation is of the Lord

KEY VERSE – 1:18

NUMBER OF CHAPTERS – 66

The Book lends itself to threefold division and the following is suggested as a helpful analysis:

| The Condemnation | This section is concerned with prophecies regarding Judah, Israel and the Gentile Nations | 1 – 35 |
| Historical Section | This contains the story of Assyrian defeat and Hezekiah's prayer, folly and punishment | 36 – 39 |

The Consolation	40 – 66
• The People of God Comforted	40 – 48
• The Suffering Servant of the Lord	49 – 57
• The Future Glory	58 – 66

The above three sections can be summed up as follows: Prophetic – Historic – Messianic

Isaiah's writing has been named 'The Gospel According to Isaiah' and has been called the most evangelical book of the Old Testament. Likewise Isaiah has been referred to as the fifth evangelist. These names at once reveal the nature of the contents and it is in this Book that there is set forth more markedly than elsewhere in the Old Testament the grace of God. Chapter 53 is an outstanding chapter and one with which no doubt you are already familiar and possibly you know most of it by heart. In this chapter there is vividly set forth the sufferings of the Lord Jesus. Particularly observe verses 3-6.

There are however many other direct references to the Lord, as for instance, to His Herald – 40:3-8; to His birth – 7:14 and 9:6; earthly lineage – 11:1; His anointing – 11:2; His Character – 11:3-5; His simple manner of life – 7:15; His ministry – 42:1-4; His death – 53; His resurrection – 25:8; His future reign of glory – 11:3-6; chapter 53 and other later chapters. In the Book of Isaiah will be found a very full portrait of the Suffering Servant of the Lord Who was to make salvation available.

One of the most frequent phrases to be found in this book is 'The Holy One of Israel' or 'The Holy One.' It occurs over 30 times and in this connection read the familiar 6:2. The vision Isaiah had of the Lord never left him.

You will find it helpful to take a concordance and to look up the various references to the word 'Salvation.' It is used in the Psalms but not frequently elsewhere in the Old Testament except in the Book of Isaiah, but here it is the key word.

There are seven 'everlastings' spoken of in Isaiah; Judgment – 33:14; Strength – 26:4; Joy – 35:10; Salvation 45:17; Kindness – 54:8; Covenant – 55:3; Light – 60:19.

Observe also the references and teaching concerning the Holy Spirit in the following verses – 10:27; 11:2; 32:15; 40:7 & 13; 42:1; 44, 3; 59:19 & 21; 61:1; 63:10.

The Book is designed to bring comfort to the People of God. Therefore observe the following references to comfort – 40:1; 43:1-2; 50:10; 51:3 & 12; 61:2,3; 63:9; 66:13. Compare chapter 50:10. Observe the three 'blesseds' – 30:18; 32:20; 56:2. Who is blessed? What is blessed activity?

In connection with Israel observe the reference to the salvation of the Remnant – 1:25-27; 2:2-3; 6:13; 11:11; 18:7; 27:12-13 and later chapters.

The last 27 chapters; namely from 40-66 have been subdivided into three sections, each of 9 chapters. Observe the following three endings – 48:22; 57:21; and 66:24.

Attention has been drawn to the fact that each of these three divisions may be subdivided once more and that chapter 53 is the central chapter of the central section of the central division. The central verses of this well-known chapter are verses 5 and 6 which contain such vital gospel truth.

In your reading and study, mark the outstanding passages, some of which will already be familiar to you but be on the lookout for spiritual gems in our reading, as for instance, 1:18; 6:1-8; 7:14; 8:20; 9:6-7. So one could go right on through the Book picking out particular portions. Observe the small but mighty chapter 12 and again your attention is directed to 53. Take time to allow the opening verses of 40-42 to speak to you afresh. This is a prophecy which cannot be read quickly or lightly, but the more time you give to meditate over its glorious truths so much the greater will be your spiritual enrichment.

QUESTIONS

1. Give the references of the historical portions in the Old Testament which are related to the period of Isaiah's ministry and the approximate time this period covers with dates.

2. When did Isaiah receive his vision of the glory of the Lord and where is this recorded?

3. What does the name 'Isaiah' mean?

4. State how you would briefly reply to the criticism that the latter part of the Book of Isaiah was written at a later date by a different author.

5. Give the Key Word, Key Phrase, Key Verse and number of chapters of this book.

6. Give a brief analysis of the book under three headings.

7. By what other names has this prophecy in the Old Testament been called?

8. What phrases or words are used with frequency in this book?

9. In which chapter is the Lord Jesus set forth as the suffering Servant?

JEREMIAH

'Operation 39' – Lesson 24

This Book contains 32 chapters and will require careful and thoughtful reading. The prophecies are not set out in their chronological order and while no doubt in the first instance you will read the Book through chapter by chapter yet a second and profitable method of reading would be as far as possible to read the prophecies in their chronological order. Paragraph 5 below will give you some idea of the chronological sequence of the various prophecies. The historic background will assist very greatly to an understanding of Jeremiah, the man and his message. You are therefore referred to the history of his times found in 2 Kings 22:1-25, 30 and to 2 Chronicles 34:1-36, 21. The period covered would be a little over 40 years, approximately 630 – 585 or 4 and covers the closing years of the Kingdom of Judah prior to the exile and overlapping a year or two into the exilic period. It was during this time that first the Assyrian power was in the ascendancy to be followed by the Babylonian Empire.

In all probability Jeremiah's contemporaries were Zephaniah, Habakkuk and Obadiah who prophesied in Judah and during the closing years of Jeremiah's ministry Ezekiel and Daniel would have been with the captives in Babylon. Daniel would have been a young prince coming to position and favor in Nebuchadnezzar's Court.

Jeremiah's ministry extended over the reign of five kings of Judah; firstly in the reign of Josiah. No doubt it was mainly as a result of Jeremiah's influence that there was the revival during the reign of Josiah. The other kings were Jehoahaz, Jehoiakim, Jehoiachin and Zedekiah. It will be seen that Jeremiah lived and ministered during one of the darkest periods in the history of the people of God preceding their being taken into captivity and during the first years of their exile in Babylon.

It was during this revival that the Book of the Law was found as recorded in 2 Kings 22. This resulted in the revival; or more strictly, reformation but this was to a large extent only superficial and with the death of Josiah there was renewed idolatry.

From the Book of Jeremiah we have an insight into the character of the man Jeremiah and probably we have more personal details of this prophet than of any of the other prophets of the Old Testament. Jeremiah was born a Priest and was called to be a Prophet in early life as is recorded in chapter 1:1-10. He was the son of Hilkiah of the priests that were in Anathoth in the land of Benjamin just north of Jerusalem. When he was called to be a prophet he pleaded that he was young and inexperienced and not able to speak – see 1:6. He did however have the assurance that the Lord had called him and set him aside to this particular work prior to his birth. With the divine anointing and commission – 1:9-10 – he went forth to his unenviable task of preaching to a rebellious and idolatrous people calling them to repentance and by reason of their non-repentance having a message of judgment to proclaim to them. From chapter 16 we discover that he was commanded not to marry for his life, as well as his words, was to be a message of rebuke to the people of God who had gone so far away from the Lord. Even members of his own family treated him treacherously and believed not his message – ch. 12:6. Likewise the men of his native city, Anathoth, refused to accept the message of the Lord that he brought – 11:21-23. There was opposition from the people – 1:17; 13:15-17; 15:20-21. There was a conspiracy against Jeremiah in Judah and Jerusalem – 18:18-23. Later we read in chapter 20:1-6 how Jeremiah was put in the stocks that were in the high gate of Benjamin by the Temple of Jerusalem – 20:2. The Princes of Judah, together with the Priests and Prophets (untrue prophets) sought to have Jeremiah put to death. Later we read of further imprisonment in chapter 37:11-21 and he was cast into a dungeon in chapter 38:1-28.

After Jerusalem had been captured by Nebuchadnezzar Jeremiah was released by order of Nebuchadnezzar, but later he was taken against his will by Johanan into Egypt with others of the remnant that had been left in Judah and there according to tradition he was later stoned to death. If there was any man who knew what it was to experience opposition from all quarters – from his own family, from his friends, from those to whom he ministered and from the people generally it was Jeremiah. No wonder he was called 'the Weeping Prophet'! From his writing it is apparent that although the message he was commissioned to proclaim was a solemn call to repentance and a stern warning of coming judgment, yet he himself was a tender-hearted and sensitive man of God. Only such a one could declare the message that was committed to him with compassion and yet do so faithfully. He had abundant cause for tears – see 9:1. Both the man and his message reveal the compassion and suffering of the Savior and the compassion of God the Father for His wandering children – see Lamentations 1:12.

Here in this writing then there is what amounts to an autobiography of the prophet himself for young though he was, timid, sensitive, sympathetic and of a retiring disposition, he nevertheless stood forth and declared with unflinching faithfulness against every opposition the message that God had commissioned him to proclaim. He has been variously called 'The weeping prophet,' 'the prophet of the broken heart,' 'the grandest man of Old Testament history.'

MEMORIZE THE FOLLOWING DETAILS

KEY WORD – Return !

KEY VERSES – 3:14 & 22; 31:2

THEME – warning of the certainty of God's judgment on sin coupled with a plea to return to the God of infinite and everlasting love and tenderness.

NUMBER OF CHAPTERS – 52

The Book combines personal details with history and prophecy and has been stated above that it is not written in chronological order but the writing seems to be grouped according to certain subjects.

The following is a brief Analysis:

Call, Consecration and Commission of the prophet	1:1-19
The Prophet's Ministry and Message	
• Ministry in General	2 – 17
• The Great Illustration	18 & 19
• Jeremiah made to Suffer	19
• The Ministry to Kings and People	21 – 45
• The Further Ministry after the Fall of Jerusalem	46 - 51
Historic Fulfillment of the Message and Judgment upon Jerusalem and Judah	52

An attempt to set out the contents in chronological order according to the reigns of the kings, the Fall of Jerusalem and subsequent events is as follows:

I. Call, Consecration and Commission of the Prophet – 1:1-19.

II. Prophecies and Events in the reign of Josiah – 2:1 – 12:17.

Prophecies and Events in the reign of Jehoikim – ch. 26; 46 – 49:33; 25; 36:1-8; 45; 36:9-32; 14; 15; 16; 17; 18 – 19:13; 19:14 – 20:18; 35; 22 – 23:40.

III. Prophecies and Events in the reign of Zedekiah – ch. 24; 27; 28; 29; 49:34-51; 21; 34; 37; 38; 39:15-18; 32; 33; 30; 31; 39:1-14.

IV. Prophecies to the Remnant in Judah – chs. 40 – 43:3.

V. Prophecies to the Remnant in Egypt: ch. 43:4 – 44:30.

VI. The Destruction of Jerusalem and Captivity of Judah – ch. 52:1-34.

Nos. I to IV took place PRIOR to the Fall of Jerusalem and Nos. V and VI took place AFTER the Fall of Jerusalem.

Judged by outward results the ministry of Jeremiah would appear to be a dismal failure but one of the outstanding lessons to be learned from this Book is that the servant of the Lord is called to be faithful irrespective of seemingly outward success or otherwise. Therefore, true success is only to be found in submitting to and doing the will of the Lord. In Christian service there is much that appears outwardly to be a failure but which earns the approval of the Lord because of its faithfulness and submission to His will.

In your reading and study of this Book observe the following words and phrases which are used with frequency:

'rising up early and speaking' – this is a vivid phrase used to emphasize the urgency and persistence of the Lord in seeking to call His people back to Himself. This is found eleven times and the only other place in which we find it is 2 Chronicles 36:15, and no doubt there the writer borrowed the phrase from The Book of Jeremiah.

'forsake and forsaken' – used 24 times.

'backslide and backsliding' – used 13 times, but only found elsewhere in the Old Testament once in Proverbs and three times in Hosea.

'return' – used 47 times.

Observe the unique phrases 'the generation of his wrath' – 7:29, and the telling phrase used to indicate the guilt of the people and their leaders and their shamelessness 'neither could they blush' – 8:12.

Observe the Lord's tender reference to His people 'the dear beloved of the Lord's heart.'

In an earlier paragraph reference has been made to the character of Jeremiah and the Book will be found to be interspersed with his prayers revealing that he was a true man of prayer, for instance, see chapter 10; 12:1-4; 14:7-8 & 11:20-21; 15:15-18; 17:13-18; 18:19-23; 20:7; 32:16-25.

There are to be found many jewels of truth in this book the thread of which is sometimes difficult to follow. Be on the lookout for these in our study and mark them so that they stand out, as for instance, 2:13; 2:21-22; 6:16; 8:20 (what a Scripture for a harvest-thanksgiving service!); 9:23-24; 10:23; 13:23; 14:8-9; 15:16; 17:9-10; 18:1-6; 23:5-6; 23:29; 31:3; 31:15; 31:31-34; 33:3.

The weeping prophet must have had a great reward when he arrived in the presence of Jehovah, His Lord and Savior. He was truly named Jeremiah for the name mans 'he whom God appoints.'

LAMENTATIONS

'Operation 39' – Lesson 25

This short Book of five poems will repay reading and rereading bearing in mind that each chapter is one complete poem.

The title is self-explanatory. It is found in the Hebrew Bible in the Hagiographa and is one of the Five Rolls or 'Megilloth.' It is read in Jewish Synagogues on the Fast held on 9th August. This day is set apart as a special day of mourning and when the Jews were able to go to the Wailing Wall in Jerusalem many would there chant the Lamentations every Friday.

The Lamentations were written by Jeremiah following the siege and fall of Jerusalem. In the Septuagint the writing is prefaced with these words 'And it came to pass after Israel was taken captive and Jerusalem made desolate that Jeremiah sat weeping and lamented with this lamentation over Jerusalem and said…' and then follows the Book as we have it. According to tradition, Jeremiah sat in a cave known as Jeremiah's Grotto on the face of the Hill of Calvary outside the City Wall. There the Prophet, looking over the ruined city was moved by the Lord to write this deeply moving lamentation over the city which had had such opportunity and privilege, but which now lay in ruins. This tradition is very telling for while it reveals the sorrow of the prophet yet it is intended to reveal the greater sorrow of the Lord Himself who later came and not only shed His tears over this same city but shed His blood on the Hill of Calvary for the sins of His people and indeed for the sin of the whole world.

The Book is composed of five poems. They are set forth in typical Hebrew form using the acrostic method as an aid to memorization. The Poems or Songs or Lamentations correspond to the chapter divisions. The Lamentations 1:2 and 4 each have 22 verses corresponding to the Hebrew alphabet of 22 letters. Each verse begins with one of the letters of the Hebrew alphabet in order, for example verse 1 commences with 'a', verse 2 with 'b' and so on. Lamentations 3 found in chapter 3 has 66 verses and instead of one verse commencing with a letter of the Hebrew alphabet, three verses each commence with the same letter; for example, verses 1-3 commence with 'a', verses 4-6 commence with 'b' and so on. The 5th Lamentation is in the form of a prayer and while there are 22 verses, the acrostic is not pursued. While in the 1st, 2nd and 3rd Lamentation each verse has three clauses it is in the 3rd Lamentation that each clause of each verse commences with the same letter. The 4th Lamentation is in couplets. These details can only be clearly discerned in the Hebrew.

Each Lamentation ends with a prayer with the exception of the 4th and this is followed by the 5th, the whole of which is a Prayer.

MEMORIZE THE FOLLOWING DETAILS

KEY WORD – Sorrow

KEY VERSE – 1:12; 2:17; 3:22-23; 4:1-2; 5:1

NUMBER OF CHAPTERS – 5

As has already been stated above, this Book reveals more than the sorrow of the prophet over Zion. It reveals the love and sorrow of the Lord Himself before His own whom He has chastened so that He might bring them back to obedience and to His purposes. Thus in a very real way, the love of God is made known through the prophet. If you refer back to the second paragraph in Lesson 24 giving details of Jeremiah it will be seen how God could only express Himself in this way through a man who was as tenderhearted and full of compassion as was the prophet. Refer to the following passages which have particular reference to Christ: 1:12; 2:15; 3:14, 15, 19, 30.

L.A.T. VAN DOOREN

The following Analysis is in accordance with the five Lamentations:

Zion the City of God portrayed as a Weeping Widow	1
Zion the City of God represented as a Veiled Woman	2
Zion the City of God represented by the Weeping Prophet	3
Zion the City of God represented as Gold become dim – the Glory has Departed	4
Zion the City of God pleads in Prayer unto the Lord	5

Here then is set forth in telling form the sorrow and misery that sin brings both to those who have sinned as well as to the heart of God Himself. It also reveals the infinite love and compassion of the Lord even when He is dealing in chastisement with His own. In this connection read Hebrews 12:1-13 and particularly verse 11.

Possibly the most precious verses of the whole book are chapter 3:22-23. These should be memorized. Thank God for His faithfulness! Remember the child of God cannot sin without bringing sorrow into his or her own life – and sorrow to the heart of the Lord.

QUESTIONS ON THE LAMENTATIONS OF JEREMIAH

1. Where is this Book found in the Hebrew Bible?

2. By whom was the Book written and what was the particular occasion which prompted the writing thereof?

3. Is there any peculiar characteristic which is discernible in the original writing?

4. Give the Key Word, Key Verse for each poem and number of chapters.

5. Give one or two references or verses which have particular reference to Christ.

6. Give a brief Analysis of the Book or state how the prophet portrays the City of God.

EZEKIEL

'Operation 39' – Lesson 26

Reading the Book of Ezekiel right through will not be an easy task, and you are advised to read according to the main divisions set out in a later paragraph. In addition you will find it helpful to refer to the portions that give the historic background to Ezekiel and his times; namely, 2 Kings chapter 24, verse 1 to chapter 25, verse 30, and 2 Chronicles chapter 36, verses 9 – 21.

This Book belongs to the writings of the Exilic Period of the Babylonian Captivity. The approximate period covered is 22 years from 594 to 572 B.C., that is, from the fifth year of the captivity of Jehoiachin. There is reference in chapter 40, verse 1 to the twenty-fifth year of Jehoiachin's captivity. Your attention is directed to the following references in each case relating to the time of Jehoiachin's captivity. Chapter 1:2; chapter 8:1; chapter 20:1; chapter 24:1; chapter 26:1; chapter 29:17; chapter 30:20; chapter 31:1; chapter 32:1; chapter 40:1. It will be seen, therefore, that the greater part of the Book is in chronological order, and is dated very much like a diary.

The Author and Prophet is Ezekiel, who, like Jeremiah, was a priest. The name 'Ezekiel' mans 'He whom God strengthens' or 'Strengthened by God.' Ezekiel as a young man was taken captive at the time of Jehoiachin's captivity, and brought with the other captives into Babylon. If, as it would appear to be in chapter 1, verse 1, the reference to the 30th year refers to the age of the Prophet, it will be seen that as this was also the fifth year of Jehoiachin's captivity, then Ezekiel would have been twenty-five years of age when he was taken captive. He was contemporary with the latter half of the Prophet Jeremiah's ministry. Daniel would have been a young man rising to a positon of power in the courts of Babylon. Daniel is referred to in chapter 14:14; and chapter 28:3. From chapter 8:1 it may be understood that he was allowed to dwell in his own house, and from chapter 24:18; that he was married but that his wife died suddenly at the time that Nebuchadnezzar laid siege to Jerusalem, prior to its destruction. Indeed from chapter 24:1; and then verses 15-18, it could be implied that his wife was taken from him the same day as the King of Babylon set himself against Jerusalem and God used this sad event in the life of the prophet as a sign to the captive people.

There are marked differences between the three Major Prophets and their presentation of the Triune God. Isaiah is a prophet whose chief presentation is that of the Son; Jeremiah's main presentation of God is of the Father, and Ezekiel is the prophet of the Spirit of God. It is in his book that there is the emphasis on the ministry of the Holy Spirit. As his name is Ezekiel – He whom God strengthens, it will be observed that it was the Spirit Who Strengthened and fitted him for his unenviable task of ministry to the unrepentant and rebellious captives. The differences between the prophets are noticeable in the fact that Isaiah was outstanding as a poet with flowing eloquence; Jeremiah was the preacher who pleaded in tenderness with the people, but in Ezekiel there is an abruptness and strength of utterance, coupled with vivid word pictures which both demands and enforces the attention of his hearers. God chooses and fashions a man according to the particular ministry He has prepared for him.

Ezekiel, like Jeremiah, had to contend with false prophets. Ezekiel's ministry was mainly at Tel-Abib on the river Chebar – chapter 3:15; and when you read of Ezekiel's 'visits' to Jerusalem it must be borne in mind that these were 'in the Spirit;' that is, in vision form, and thus the Spirit of God enabled him to see and interpret events transpiring in the far away capital.

In Chapters 1 – 3 you read of Ezekiel's call and the vision granted to him whereby God commissioned him to his ministry as a prophet.

In this writing Ezekiel is called the 'son of man' approximately ninety times. From the first vision in chapter 1 it will be seen that Ezekiel is called to be like the One upon the throne, who when He came in the flesh took the title 'Son of Man' to Himself.

MEMORIZE THE FOLLOWING DETAILS

KEY PHRASE – The Glory of the Lord

KEY VERSE – "This was the appearance of the likeness of the Glory of the Lord." 1:28

NUMBER OF CHAPTERS – 48

Referring back to the key phrase given above, refer to the following references and note the content of the phrase "Glory of God." Ch. 8:4; 9:3; 10:19; 11:22; 43:2

Observe the following references and note the context of the phrase "Glory of the Lord."

Ch. 1:28; 3:12; 3:23; 10:4; 10:18; 11:23; 43:4

In a vision Ezekiel saw the Glory of the Lord leave the Temple. Observe chapter 8:4; and chapter 10:1. First the Glory of the Lord removes to the threshold of the house, chapter 10:4; then passing on stood at the door of the east gate, verses 10, 18 and 19. Then from the Temple and city to Olivet 11:22 and 23. The truth thus stated is that the Glory of the Lord left both the Sanctuary of the Temple and the City made holy by His presence. Slowly, as if with reluctance, and yet with Divine Majesty, the Glory departed. It is in chapter 43 that the Glory of the Lord returns and the Book terminates with the prophecy concerning the Lord in the midst of His people and ends with the significant phrase "The Lord is there."

This movement sums up the message of the Book for after Ezekiel has been granted a vision of the Glory of the Lord and called to service, his chief ministry was to prophecy concerning the destruction of Jerusalem as a judgment upon the people of God for their sin. This prophecy also constituted a call to repentance as well as a warning against indulging in false hopes or wishful thinking. There were false prophets that are teaching that the captives would soon be restored to their own land and city. News of this travelled to Jerusalem, and in Jeremiah chapter 29 it is recorded that Jeremiah, hearing of these false prophets and their message, wrote a letter from Jerusalem exposing and denouncing the folly of such false hopes. Later Ezekiel, after having declared how the Glory of the Lord has departed from the Temple, is called upon to console, and to strengthen the people of God, to believe in God's goodness and promises of restoration to the penitent. Later he delivers the promises of future quickening by the Spirit of God, the return of the Glory of the Lord and establishment of his Presence in the midst.

The Book may be analyzed according to the chronological order of the contents:

Prophecies Prior to the Siege of Jerusalem	1 – 24
Prophecies During the Siege of Jerusalem	25 – 37
Prophecies After the Siege of Jerusalem	33 – 48

A further Analysis of the contents is as follows:

The Vision of the Glory of the Lord	1
Ezekiel Called and Commissioned	2 – 3
Departure of the Glory of the Lord	4 – 24
Judgment pronounced on Jerusalem and Judah	
The Glory of God in relation to other nations	25 – 32
Judgments are pronounced on Ammon, Moab, Edom, Philistia, Tyre, Sidon & Egypt	
The Way Prepared for Return of the Glory of the Lord	33 – 37
Judgment Pronounced upon Gog and Magog	38 – 39
The Return of the Glory of the Lord	40 - 48

The use of the following phrase should be noted:

"They shall know that I am the Lord." This is used approximately 70 times. It will be discovered that the purpose of God's judgment upon Jerusalem and His people, and also on the Gentile nations, and furthermore in connection with the restoration and final blessing of His people, is that All may know that He is the Lord God and that there is none else.

The phrase "They shall know that I am the Lord" is used:

- 29 in connection with judgment on Jerusalem
- 24 times in connection with judgment on Gentile nations
- 17 times in connection with the restoration and final blessing of the Lord's people.

Attention has been drawn, in the second paragraph to the chronological sequence and date references. The following phrase should also be noted in this connection, for they introduce the principal prophetic messages:

'The hand of the Lord was upon me' – 1:3; 3:14 & 22; 8:1; 33:22; 37:1; 40:1

Another frequent phrase introducing new messages is "and the Word of the Lord came unto me."

From these phrases and references it will be seen that Ezekiel was a man who was not only in fellowship with his Lord but upon whom the hand of the Lord was upon in a marked degree, and his ministry is characterized by the compulsion that arises out of fellowship with the thrice Holy God who is glorious in all His ways and Works.

Your attention is specially directed to the following chapters:

34 – Woe is pronounced to the unfaithful shepherds and then in contrast there is presented a picture of the Good Shepherd.

36 – This chapter has been called the "Gospel according to Ezekiel." It contains tender and precious promises. Particularly note verses 25-27.

37 – The resurrection of dry bones under the breath of the Spirit.

47 – The vision of the rivers of living water.

While it is recognized that these prophecies may have particular and special application to Israel, the spiritual principles they contain may be applied to the people of God, and to Christians individually, for in Christ there is cleansing, a new heart, a new life and a new power available in the indwelling Holy Spirit. His presence is sufficient to meet every need and to fulfill the Lord's purpose in His own.

QUESTIONS

1. What does the name Ezekiel mean?
2. State to which period of Hebrew history Ezekiel and his writing belong.
3. Which Prophets were contemporary with Ezekiel?
4. Each of the three Major Prophets emphasized one person of the Trinity. What is Ezekiel's main emphasis?
5. State the Key Phrase, Key Verse and number of Chapters of the book of Ezekiel.
6. Write out a brief Analysis of the Book according to the chronological sequence of events.
7. Mention one or two important phrases that are used in this Book.
8. State briefly the contents of chapter 37.
9. State briefly the contents of chapter 47.

DANIEL

'Operation 39' – Lesson 27

It is not a formidable task to read through the whole of the twelve chapters of the Book of Daniel. If you are unable to do this without interruption, then it is suggested that you read it through according to the two main divisions given later. The portions in the Historical Books of the Old Testament corresponding to the times of Daniel are 2 Kings 23:36 to 25:30 and 2 Chronicles 36:5-23. The approximate date would be 606 to 534 B.C.

The Book and Prophecy of Daniel belong to the Exilic Period of Hebrew history.

In the Hebrew Bible the Book of Daniel is not included among the Prophets but is one of the books in the Kethubim or Latter Writings. In the English Bible Daniel is included in the Prophetic section by reason of the Apocalyptic nature of his writing although Daniel himself is not usually considered a Prophet within the customary meaning of the word.

The name Daniel means "God is my Judge" or alternatively "Judged of God." These interpretations find fulfillment in the life and character of Daniel for God vindicated His servant on the one hand and also used him whereby to deliver judgment in the name of the Lord.

It will be helpful to understand something of the historic background to the Book, hence the above references in 2 Kings and 2 Chronicles. Daniel with his friends were taken to Babylon by Nebuchadnezzar, who came against Judah and Jerusalem three times. The first occasion;

about 606 B.C. when King Jehoiakim, Daniel, his friends and others were taken captive. Nebuchadnezzar came against Judah the second time in approximately 598 B.C. when King Jehoiachin was taken captive. Ezekiel was among the captives at this time. In 588 B.C. Nebuchadnezzar came against Jerusalem for the third and last time, destroying the city and temple. At this time, King Zedekiah was taken prisoner and carried away into captivity.

Daniel is thought to have been a member of the Royal house, and certainly he was a Prince of Judah. He was probably about 16 years of age when he was taken captive. He and his friends are referred to as children in 1:4. He lived throughout the Babylonian period on into the reign of Cyrus the Persian, 1:21, and this would cover a period of at least 70 years, so it is probable that he was a man of about 90 years of age when he died. As you will read in chapter 1, he was set aside in preparation and entered into Court life in the Royal Palaces at Babylon and Shushan. There is no doubt that there was much wickedness and evil in such surroundings but amidst it all Daniel lived a holy sanctified life. He stood true to the Lord God, giving Him the first place in his heart and life. Nevertheless, he rose to occupy the highest position in the state, and exercised a powerful political influence in the Babylonian and Medo-Persian Empires. In Ezekiel 14:20 and 28:3, Daniel is referred to in company with Noah and Job by reason of his righteous and godly manner of living. The testimony of his enemies is to be found in 6:5.

In 2:1, Nebuchadnezzar's dream, which Daniel interpreted, is stated to be in the second year of that monarch's reign. The last recorded vision of Daniel was in the third year of Cyrus and between these two dates there is a period of 70 years; 3:10.

From the dates it will, therefore, be seen that he had several Prophets as contemporaries – Zephaniah was terminating his ministry and Jeremiah was still prophesying in Jerusalem, and probably Habakkuk likewise and Obadiah. Ezekiel was contemporary with him in Babylon.

In your reading of this Book you will observe that chapters 1-6 are written in the third person and chapters 7-12 are written in the first person. This in itself does not detract from accepting that Daniel was the writer of the whole of the Book. Chapter 1:1 – chapter 2:3; and chapter 8:1 – chapter 12:13, are written in Hebrew. Chapters 2:4 – chapter 7:28 are written in Aramaic.

MEMORIZE HE FOLLOWING DETAILS

KEY PHRASE – "The Most High Rules in the kingdom of men"

THEME – The Sovereignty of God

KEY VERSES – 2:20-22

NUMBER OF CHAPTERS – 12

OUTSTANDING CHAPTER – 9

The Book may be divided into two sections; the first written in the third person dealing with Historical matters and the second being Prophetical and written in the first person. They are as follows:

I. Historical	1 – 6
• Daniel in the reign of Nebuchadnezzar	1 – 4
• Daniel in the reign of Belshazzar	5
• Daniel in the reign of Darius	6
II. Prophetical	7 – 12
• The Vision of the Four Beasts	7
• The Vision of the Ram and He-goat	8
• Daniel's Prayer & Vision of 70 weeks	9
• The Vision of the Lord	10
• Further Prophecies concerning the Time of the End	11
• Final Words of Encouragement to Daniel	12

There is no doubt that Daniel is the great apocalyptic Prophet of the Old Testament. His prophecies deal with world empires and particularly "The Times of the Gentiles." It is a Book which is the key to later prophecies concerning the second coming of Christ, and to which the Lord Himself refers in Matthew 24:15. Incidentally, in this reference it is seen that the Lord accepted this prophecy as being made by His servant Daniel and He applies to Himself the title 'Son of Man,' thereby accepting the reference in 7:13 as being to Himself.

While the Book is remembered chiefly on account of its prophetic message, it has much other valuable teaching, not to mention the thrilling events of the earlier chapters, such as Daniel's three friends being tried by fire, the scene at the feast of Belshazzar, and Daniel being cast into the den of lions. From these and other portions of the Book it is made clear that to stand true to the purposes of God is to enter into the blessing of God, and that this often results in a measure of material and earthly prosperity in this life. See for instance 1:8 & 20; 2, 48 & 49; 3:30.

Here too, it will be seen that those who trust in the Lord and seek Him in prayer and humility are entrusted by God with spiritual discernment, and indeed the secret of the Lord. Compare 2:19, 22 & 47, and 5:11 with Psalm 25:14.

In chapter 3 there is a very telling illustration of the abiding presence of the Lord to comfort and sustain in time of particular need 3:25. Compare with further amplification of this truth – Hebrews 13:5 & 6.

Your attention is specially directed to Daniel's intercessory prayer recorded in Chapter 9. This is one of the great prayers of Scripture.

It is impossible to read this Book through without being warned against the sin and folly of pride, and of disregarding the warnings and judgments of God. See for instance chapter 4:30-37, and 5:22-31.

Link the following two phrases and think them over. Daniel 1:8 "But Daniel purposed in his heart that he would not defile himself…" with Daniel 1:21 "And Daniel continued…"

QUESTIONS

1. Give the approximate date of the Book of Daniel.
2. Name three of the twelve rulers who exercised power during the times of Daniel.

3. Give the meaning of the name 'Daniel.'

4. Give the following details of the Book of Daniel: Key Phrase, Theme, Key Verses, Number of Chapters

5. Chapter 9 has been referred to as an outstanding chapter in this Book. Why?

6. Name other Prophets which were contemporary with the times of Daniel.

7. Give a brief twofold Division of the Book.

8. Which particular incident or verses have been of greatest help and blessing to you as you have read the Book? State why.

HOSEA

'Operation 39' – Lesson 28

Take time to read through the whole of the Book of the Prophet Hosea. It is a writing that does not lend itself to quick reading. In addition, refer to the historic background to the life and times of Hosea found in 2 Kings 15:1 – 18:2. The Book and Prophecy of Hosea belongs to the Pre-exilic period of Hebrew history.

It will be seen from Hosea 1:1 that the prophet lived and prophesied during the reigns of Uzziah, Jothan, Ahaz and Hezekiah, kings of Judah and during the reigns of Jeroboam, the son of Joash, king of Israel. This latter is Jeroboam the Second. From this reference, it suggests that Hosea prophesied longer than any other prophet, probably covering a period of 72 years. Thus it will be seen that even if he commenced his prophetic ministry at an early age he must have died when he was in his 90's.

Hosea is one of the three prophets of the Northern Kingdom comprised of the Ten Tribes of Israel, the other two prophets being Jonah and Amos, who were contemporary with him. Also among his contemporaries, as prophets to the Southern Kingdom of Judah, were Joel, Isaiah and Micah – although the latter prophet ministered also to both kingdoms.

The name Hosea means "Salvation." It is identical in derivation and in meaning with the names Oshea, Jehoshua, Joshua (Numbers 13:8 & 16 and 14:6) and Jesus (Matthew 1:21).

As you will discover in your reading of the Book, the Ten Tribes are not only addressed under the name 'Israel' as a nation but also under the name of Ephraim. This latter name is used about 35 times in the Book. The reason for this is that Ephraim was the most influential and powerful of the Ten Tribes and the one that was largely responsible for departure from the pure worship of the Lord. It was from the tribe of Ephraim that Jeroboam first came. He is referred to as the one 'who made Israel to sin.' 1 Kings 15:26. Likewise the nation is also referred to as 'Samaria' as that was the Northern Kingdom's capital city.

Apart from Chapter 1:1-11 and Chapter 3:1-5, the whole of the Book is written in poetical form and contains many striking metaphors which enforce its message. It has been called one of the most profound and spiritual books of the prophets.

MEMORIZE THE FOLLOWING DETAILS

KEY WORD – Return!

KEY VERSES – 14:1 & 4

NUMBER OF CHAPTERS – 14

OUTSTANDING CHAPTER – 14

In the opening chapters of the Book you read of the personal tragedy in the home of Hosea the prophet and the names of the children have prophetic significance.

Jezreel God will scatter

Lo-ruhamah Not having obtained mercy

Lo-ammi Not my people

The story of the faithlessness of his wife and of how the prophet went and sought her again and drew her back to himself is made the basis of his message to the sinning nation of Israel.

A simple Division of the Book, based upon the personal tragedy and the national tragedy is as follows:

I. The Personal Tragedy in the Home of the Prophet	1:1 – 3:5
• A faithless wife	
• A faithful and forgiving husband	
II. The National Tragedy by Reason of the Sin of God's People	4:1 – 14:9
• The faithless nation	
• The faithful and forgiving Lord	

The following is also suggested as an Analysis of the contents of the Book.

The Sin of the People Laid Bare	1:1 – 7:16
The Resulting Judgment upon Sin	8:1 – 10:15
The Grace and Love of the Lord Revealed in the Wooing and Restoration of the Nation	11:1 - 9

In an earlier paragraph attention has been drawn to the meanings of the names Lo-ruhamah and Lo-ammi – meaning 'not having obtained mercy' and 'not my people', respectively. Observe also the reference in chapter 2:1 to the message contained within the names 'Ammi,' meaning 'My People' and 'Ruhamah,' meaning 'Having obtained mercy.' The message of the book may be summed up in these words:

'Lo-ammi' – 'not my people' and

'Ammi' – 'My People'

For in this writing there is set forth the holiness of God manifested against the loathsomeness of sin and the idolatry of His people. In judgment for their sin, He must cast them off as no longer usable in His purposes, but the writing also reveals the heart of the Lord which goes out in love and compassion to woo and win back His people, drawing them again to Himself by the bands of His love. Observe such passages as 2:14 & 15; 2:19 & 20. Also note chapter 3, which contains the Lord's Word to the prophet to go and seek and restore his faithless wife. Observe 6:4; 11:1, 3 & 4; 11:8 and particularly the whole of chapter 14.

This Book was written specially for a backsliding nation. Its message today is most applicable, in view of the carnal and backsliding state of the Church of Jesus Christ. It is also, nevertheless, a message to the backsliding and wandering Christian for while the sin of departure from the Lord is laid bare, yet the love and compassion of the Lord in seeking His own and declaring His love, healing and sufficiency for all those who return to Him, is abundantly set forth.

Your attention is again directed to chapter 14. It would be a good exercise to learn either the whole of this chapter or the outstanding verses by heart. It will be observed that there are several different speakers in the chapter. First of all, the prophet as the Ambassador of God, is calling upon the people to return to the Lord, verses 1-3. Then the Lord Himself is set forth as speaking directly to the people, declaring how He will heal their backsliding and love them freely, verses 4-7. Verse 8 tells how Ephraim the nation is speaking "What have I to do any more with idols?" This is followed by the Lord Himself speaking "I have heard his and observed him." Once again Ephraim speaks "I am like a green fir tree" followed by a further word from the Lord "From me is thy fruit found." The chapter concludes with the prophet speaking once again, verse 9.

In the Prophecy of Hosea there is set forth a great message on Sin, Judgment and Love – the Sin of departing from God, the inevitable Judgment that follows as the consequence of such sin and the infinite, unmerited free Love of God that ever seeks to heal and restore His wandering people and His wandering child. Here is set forth Sin – Judgment – Love, the Heart and Holiness of the Lord.

JOEL

'Operation 39' – Lesson 29

Read the Book of Joel through more than once during the course of this study. You are also referred to the probable historic background to the times of Joel, to be found in 2 Kings 11 & 12 and 2 Chronicles 24 & 25.

The Book and Prophecy of Joel belongs to the Pre-exilic Period of Hebrew history.

The name Joel means "Jehovah; i.e., The Lord is God" or "The Lord is my God." There are a number of men in the Bible names Joel but none of these appear to refer to the Prophet, and no personal details are known of Joel the Prophet other than the description given in 1:1. In that verse, he declares his authority and the name of his father. The obvious inference from his prophecy is that he lived in Judea and probably in Jerusalem.

Joel is usually considered to be one of the earliest, if not the earliest of the Writing Prophets, and as shown by the references quoted above from Kings and Chronicles, he exercised his ministry in the early days of the reign of Joash in which case he would almost certainly have known both Elijah and Elisha. Joel is looked upon as The Pioneer of the Writing Prophets, and the theme of his message underlines all written Hebrew prophecy. He has also been called "A Proclaimer of Judgment" and his writing "A Call to National Repentance." These phrases indicate something of the nature of the contents of the Book.

A more recent view concerning authorship, and date, is that it was written in the post-exilic period, the 4th Century or even later but there seems to be no valid reason for accepting this more recent view instead of the traditional view concerning the date of Joel's prophecy.

The action and subsequent events recorded in 2 Chronicles 24:15-24 may have been the background of Joel's message.

The Prophet Amos can be more certainly dated; see Amos 1:1, and he uses a phrase of Joel's as his test, thereby suggesting that Joel was prior to Amos. Compare Joel 3:16 with Amos 1:2.

MEMORIZE THE FOLLOWING DETAILS

KEY WORD – Visitation

KEY PHRASE – The Day of the Lord

KEY VERSE – 1:15

NUMBER OF CHAPTERS – 3

The Book may be divided as follows:

I. Historic Events	1:1 – 2:17
From these the Prophet gives warning	
II. Prophetic Utterances	2:18 – 3:21
By these the Prophet promises deliverance and blessing through repentance and final restoration	

A Fuller Analysis of the Book is as follows

I. Desolation – the Sign of Judgment	1:1 – 2:12
• The Cause – The Locust	1:4
• The Call – to all to awake and cry unto the Lord	1:5-14
• The Completeness of the Judgment – even to beasts on earth	1:15-20
• The Coming of the Judgment – the trumpet to sound alarm	2:1-11
II. Repent and Turn to the Lord	2:12-17

• The Call to Repentance	2:12-13a
• The Character of the Lord your God	2:13a-14
• The Call to Pray	2:15-17
III. Deliverance and Restoration	2:18 – 3:21
• Present Blessing	2:18-27
• Restoration and Recovery of Joy	
• Future Blessing	2:28 – 3:21
• Outpouring of the Spirit	2:28-32
• Vanquishing of all enemies	3:1-17
• The Lord in the midst	3:18-21

The Key Phrase, as stated, is "The Day of the Lord." This is found in the following references:

1:15; 2:1; 2:11; 2:31; 3:14

In 2:2 and 3:18 there are references to that day, meaning the Day of the Lord. Refer to these verses and consider carefully their different applications.

There is a vivid description in chapter 2 of the locust invasion which brought ruin in its train. This forms the immediate occasion of the Prophecy. It is made clear by such scriptures as Deuteronomy 28:38 and 1 Kings 8:37, that the plagues of locusts would be one of the ways in which God would chastise and speak to His people but this appears to have been overlooked in the time of Joel. There is no reason for doubting that this swarm to which the Prophet refers was actual but it has also allegorical and apocalyptic significance, for it points to the invasion of the land by enemy forces and also finally to the judgment of the Lord to be visited upon the nations in the last days. Joel makes it clear that these natural calamities are, in reality, Divine Visitations which foreshadow and may even herald the final judgments of the Lord. Observe the Lord's reference in 2:25 – "My great army" in His description of the locusts. The reference to cankerworm, caterpillar and palmerworm probably refer to stages of development of the locust or maybe to different varieties of locusts.

Thus it is seen that the ministry of the Prophet was directed to warn the nation to interpret the signs of the times, and then to exhort to a national repentance and return to God. He forewarns of Divine Visitation in Judgment. Later, following the call to Repentance, promises Divine Visitation in Blessing by the outpoured Spirit.

An important Prophecy found in the Book is in chapter 2:28-32. This is quoted by Peter on the Day of Pentecost. See Acts 2:16-21. It has reference to the outpouring of the Holy Spirit. There are those who believe that the prophecy will also have a later fulfillment but this would seem to be inconsistent with Peter's quotation of it and furthermore it should be remembered that this present time is the Pentecostal Age which extends up to the Lord's Second Coming. This event will be preceded by signs in the heavens and the ushering in of the Day of the Lord in Judgment. As there were ecstatic signs at the beginning of the Pentecostal Age, so there will be the Judgment signs at its close.

Your attention is drawn to the state of blessing which is foretold in 3:18-21. This scripture would appear to point to the coming blessing that awaits Israel in the Day of the Lord.

Also observe the following outstanding passages: 2:12-14; 2:25-27; 2:28-32 (these verses have already been referred to above). 3:13-15 – in connection with this scripture it should be noted that the decision is the Lord's! The reference to harvest in this chapter should be compared with Matthew 13:36-43 and Revelation 14:18-20.

Compare the following scriptures – Joel 2:13; Matthew 27:51; Isaiah 64:1. The Prophecy of Joel is a call to repentance with the promise of restoration and outpoured blessing. The sequence of the three scriptures quoted above suggest that as the heart is truly rent in Repentance, so there is immediate Access to God through the rent Veil, resulting in the Fullness of the outpoured Holy Spirit from Heaven. Joel points the way to true revival to the Church of Jesus Christ as well as to the individual Believer.

QUESTIONS

1. Suggest one or two names that have been applied to the Prophet Joel and his writing.

2. Give the meaning of the name Joel.

3. Give the Key Word, Key Phrase, Key Verse and number of Chapters of the Book.

4. What natural calamity is used by the Prophet as a sign of coming Judgment?

5. Sum up the message of the Book in three or four words or short phrases.

6. Which prophecy is of outstanding importance and was quoted by Peter as recorded in Acts chapter 2?

7. Analyze the Book under two short headings.

AMOS

'Operation 39' – Lesson 30

In addition to reading through the nine chapters of the Book of the Prophet Amos you should refer to the historic background of the Prophet and his writing to be found in 2 Kings 14:23 – 15:7, and 2 Chronicles 26. Amos was a Pre-Exilic Prophet.

The date and period the of the Book is contained in Amos 1:1 where reference is made to Uzziah, King of Judah and Jeroboam II, King of Israel. It is also stated that Amos prophesied two years before the earthquake. The earthquake must have been with some considerable severity for Zechariah refers to this event 300 or so years later (Zechariah 14:5). The following references in the Book tell of this coming earthquake: 5:8; 6:11; 8:8; 9:5

Amos was contemporary with the Prophet Joel in the South and with Jonah and later Hosea in the North. Isaiah and Micah, later Prophets to Judah would probably have been young men while Amos was alive.

The name Amos means "Weighty" or "Burden." He came from the town of Tekoa – a desert town in the hill country of Judea, twelve miles from Jerusalem, but although a citizen of the kingdom of Judah, Amos prophesied against the Kingdom of Israel, that is the Northern Kingdom, in all probability at Bethel – see 7:10.

The pastoral surroundings in which Amos was brought up are reflected in the man and his ministry. He describes himself as a herdsman; that is one who no doubt looked after the goats, sheep and cattle and also a gatherer of wild figs – 7:14. The latter phrase refers to the very humble occupation of being a dresser or pincher of the Sycamore or wild figs (also known as Egyptian figs) which were ripened by pinching and used as food by none but the very poor. Furthermore, he emphasizes to Amaziah, the priest of Bethel, that he was not one who had been trained in the School of the Prophets - 7:14. Nevertheless, although he had a very humble and lowly upbringing, he was one whom the Lord called and sent forth with a message that was full of power and he himself manifests faithfulness and courage in his ministry. The writing that you are now studying is often referred to as a classic in its style and simplicity in the Hebrew. Amos may be likened to John Bunyan, who likewise was a man of a humble and lowly upbringing, a tinker by trade but who nevertheless wrote *Pilgrim's Progress*, a classic of English literature.

In the writing there is presented a vivid picture of the times in which Amos lived. It was one of material prosperity under Uzziah in Judah, and Jeroboam II in Israel. Outward ritual was observed but there was no true regard for God as is seen by the denunciation of the sins of the people. The rich lived in luxury by oppressing the poor. It was an age of rottenness, luxury, licentiousness, robbery, lying, slavery and drunkenness. See such scriptures as 2:4-8 & 12; 3:10; 4:1; 5:7,10-12 & 26; 6:3-6; 8:4-6. Also observe 8:12 13.

At the same time note in our reading the many references to pastoral pursuits and the use of illustrations from country life. It must have been a shock for the men and women of the royal court of Samaria to be addressed in the blunt and unconventional style of the Prophet from the country – particularly when he referred to the ladies of the court as "The kine of Bashan" that is, as cows! Observe every reference to country life which Amos uses to enforce his message.

MEMORIZE THE FOLLOWING DETAILS

KEY WORD - Punishment

KEY VERSE – 4:12

KEY PHRASE – Prepare to meet thy God

NUMBER OF CHAPTERS – 9

THEME – National sin leads to judgment of the nation.

The outstanding message of the Book is that of Judgment, that is, Punishment from the Lord. The word 'Punishment' is used a number of times. In the opening part of the Book, Judgment is foretold on surrounding nations. This is followed by the warning of Judgment to come upon Judah and Israel. At the time Amos came forth, this seemed to be most unlikely hence the message was unacceptable – 7:10-13. It is particularly emphasized in the Book that privilege brings a corresponding responsibility and as, therefore, Israel had had greater privilege through God's Word the nation is warned of severer and great judgment than on the heathen nations.

The Book also makes it clear that all nations are in the Hand of God, and that God is the Lord of all – 1:2; 4:13; 5:8.

The following is a brief Analysis:

Prophetic Utterances	1:1 – 2:16
Problems Concerned with the Judgment	3:1 – 6:14
Parabolic Pictures to Enforce the Message	7:1 – 9:10
Promises of Restoration by the Lord	9:11-15

A further and fuller Analysis of the Book is as follows:

Introduction – The Prophet and his times, 1:1-2

I. Declaration of the Sin and Judgment to come on Israel's Neighbors	1:3 – 2:3
II. Declaration of the Sin and Judgment to come on Judah and Israel	2:4-16
III. Five Messages Declaring Israel's Sin and Coming Judgment	3:1 – 6:14
IV. Five Visions Declaring Israel's Sin and Coming Judgment	7:1 – 9:10
V. Declaration of Restoration by the Lord	9:11-15

In connection with the Analysis in the previous paragraph, observe that under the first heading: I Declaration of the Sin and Judgment to come on Israel's Neighbors – 1:3 – 2:3; Each declaration is introduced with a note of authority by the phrase "Thus saith the Lord." Five of the six declarations are followed by the same phrase. You will also observe the expression which is repeated eight times "For three transgressions of.... And for four, I will not turn away." This is a Hebrew idiom denoting that the nation referred to has overstepped the mark of God's patience. It could be paraphrased and rendered "I have forgiven thee three transgressions but for the fourth I will visit in judgment." In three transgressions the nations had filled full their cup of iniquity and in the fourth it overflowed and judgment must follow. Compare Genesis 15-16.

Under II. Declaration of the Sin and Judgment on Judah and Israel – 2:4-16. Observe that the people of God had also filled full their iniquity – see 2:13. This is a picturesque pastoral reference. The last sheaf had been cast upon the cart!

Under III Five Messages Declaring Israel's Sin and Coming Judgment – 3: 1 – 6: 14. Observe that three of these messages commence with the phrase "Hear this Word" 3: 1; 4: 1; 5: 1; the other two with "woe" 5:18; 6:1, and in all the word "therefore" is used to denote the justice of the judgment. Because of unrighteous conduct and ignored warnings, therefore, judgment must come – 3: 2; 3:11; 4:12; 5:16; 5:27; 6:7; 8:7.

Under IV Five Visions Declaring Israel's Sin and Coming Judgment – 7: 1 – 9: 10. Observe the apt and vivid pictures that are employed. The locusts which devour 7: 1-3, the fire which consumes – 7: 4-6; the plumb-line which exposes – 7:7-11; the basket of summer fruit, ripeness for judgment – 8; the Lord by the altar for the execution of judgment – 9:1-10.

Under V The Declaration of Restoration – 9:11-15, it is equally important that you should observe the five "I will's" of the Lord. As surely as judgment is promised and comes as a result of continued departure from God, so also the Lord is faithful, who will not forsake His people and five times over He uses the phrase "I will," and three times over the phrase "saith the Lord." This is his guarantee. God is faithful!

The following are noteworthy verses which deserve particular thought:

3: 3; 3:7-8; 4:12; 6:1; 7:14-15; 8:2; 8:11; 9:13-15

An important scripture, which is also an apt summing up of the message of the Book, is the one quoted by James at the Council in Jerusalem, see Acts 15: 16-17. It is Amos 9: 11-12. Furthermore, observe Acts 15:18.

QUESTIONS

1. What natural calamity took place shortly after the time of Amos's prophecy, and where else is this referred to in the later Books of the Prophets.

2. What does the name "Amos" mean?

3. State the town from which Amos came and to which kingdom he delivered his prophecy.

4. What calling did Amos follow prior to his entering into the prophetic ministry? Is there any evidence of this calling in his Book?

5. Give the following details: Key Word, Key Verse, Key Phrase and number of chapters.

6. What is the outstanding message of the Book?

7. In one section of the Book the Prophet uses five vivid pictures to describe Israel's sin and coming judgment. What were these vivid illustrations?

8. Where in the Book of Acts, and on what occasion was there a quotation from the Book of Amos?

OBADIAH

'Operation 39' – Lesson 31

The Book of the Prophet Obadiah comprises of one short chapter of 21 verses. Read it through more than once during this study.

The name Obadiah means "Servant of Jehovah." Although there are several Obadiahs mentioned in the Old Testament, none can be identified as having written this Book, and no personal details are known of the writer.

It is almost impossible to date the Book with certainty for it has been variously placed as being the first of the Writing Prophets, with his references to the fall of Jerusalem as being an invasion which took place between the years 848 and 844 B.C. Others, place the ministry of the Prophet later in the history of Judah and, yet others, consider he uttered his prophecy shortly after the destruction of Jerusalem by Nebuchadnezzar. While it cannot be stated with certainty, yet this would seem to be the most likely date of the Prophet and his prophecy. A strong reason for this date is that following the destruction of Jerusalem, at a later date Nebuchadnezzar also ravaged the Edomites. They were further defeated and massacred in thousands by Cyrus, the King of Persia. Still later they were defeated by the Jews under the Maccabees and from then on do not appear to have existed any longer as a nation. The reference in verses 10-14 seems to indicate the destruction of Jerusalem under Nebuchadnezzar. The passages in the historic section of the Old Testament that would give the background to these events are to be found in 2 Kings 25 and 2 Chronicles 36:11-21.

Accepting the date of the Book as being related to the fall of Jerusalem in 586, it will be seen that Obadiah's prophecy belongs to the Exilic period and in all probability he prophesied in the land while Judah was in captivity.

Three of the principal enemies of the people of God were Edom, Assyria and Babylon. In each case a prophetic book is devoted to the downfall and the doom of these nations. Habakkuk deals with the doom of the Chaldeans, that is Babylon; Nahum with Ninevah, that is Assyria; and Obadiah with Edom and the Edomites.

The theme of the Book of Obadiah is "The Doom of Edom." It has even been called a "hymn of hate" against Edom but rather than that, it is much more to be considered as a 'hymn of consolation' for the people of God, in view of all that they suffered at the hands of Edom. Obadiah, the servant of Jehovah, has been called "A Minister of Consolation."

It will be remembered that the Edomites were the descendants of Esau. You can read in Genesis of the quarrel between Jacob and Esau. This quarrel is reflected in their posterity. The Edomites, also known later as the Idumeans, developed into a very fierce, bitter, proud people, ever resentful against the descendants of Jacob. Nevertheless, God commanded His people to treat the Edomites well, as for instance in Deuteronomy 2: 3-7 and 23:7. The Edomites did, however, manifest the same attitude as Esau who is referred to in Hebrews 11:16 as a profane person; that is, as an ungodly man. He was one who had no conscience, no faith and no spiritual vision or desire. Likewise, his descendants had no room or time for God, or for the people of God. In particular, the crowning set of iniquity was when Edom rejoiced over Israel's downfall and the destruction of Jerusalem and availed themselves of the opportunity to further massacre and plunder the people of God. In this connection read Psalm 137, particularly noting verse 7. Also refer to Lamentations 4:21-22. Destruction is pronounced upon Edom even though the Edomites boast themselves of their security and the impregnability of their rock dwellings – verse 3. Nevertheless, God says they will be brought down – verse 4, their wives and mighty men be destroyed – verses 8 & 9, because of the violence they have shown to

Jacob and his descendants and their cruel attitude when Jerusalem was destroyed, and when they rejoiced over the destruction of Judah verses 10-13.

The Book is a confirmation of the message delivered to Abraham in Genesis 12:3, where the promise and the warning stands concerning the people of God "I will bless them that bless thee and curse him that curseth thee."

MEMORIZE THE FOLLOWING DETAILS

KEY WORD – Retribution

KEY VERSE – 15

NUMBER OF VERSES – 21

The book may be summed up in the following phrases:

Edom's Humiliation – Edom's Crime – Edom's Doom

A short Analysis is as follows:

	Verses
The Deceitful Pride and False Security of Edom	1-4
The Doom of Edom Announced	5-9
The Reasons for Edom's Coming Destruction	10-16
The Irrevocable Fall of Edom and the Certain Restoration	17-21

It is important to note that contained within this prophecy of doom, there is the promise of the restoration of the people of God. A further brief division of the Book emphasizing this could be made as follows:

I. The Overthrow of Edom – 1-16

II. The Deliverance or Triumph of Israel – 17-21

In connection with the restoration of Israel, observe the use of the word 'possess' or 'possessions.' Israel the people of God are called upon to possess their possessions. This is the Book's message to Christians, to rest in the Lord, knowing that the Lord will deal with all that the adversary does in seeking to bring low the people of God and with the Lord there is certain victory. Therefore, the Christian and the Church can go forward triumphantly.

The last phrase of the Book is significant – "The kingdom shall be the Lord's."

QUESTIONS

1. How many verses are there in the Book of Obadiah?
2. Give the meaning of the name 'Obadiah.'
3. With what particular event does the Prophet Obadiah concern himself in his prophecy?
4. Give the following details: Key Word; Key Verse.
5. Sum up the Book of Obadiah in three short phrases.
6. Do you remember the last phrase of the Book?

JONAH

'Operation 39' – Lesson 32

It will be a delight to read and reread the Book of Jonah which has been described as "the most beautiful story ever written in so few words" – but then it is more than a story! Also refer to 2 Kings 13 & 14 and 2 Chronicles 25 for the historic background of Jonah and his times. In all probability Jonah exercised his ministry just immediately prior to and during the reign of Jeroboam the Second. The approximate date of this period would be 840 – 782 B.C. and Jonah and his prophecy do, therefore, belong to the Pre-Exilic period of Hebrew history.

There is a direct reference to Jonah in 2 Kings 14: 25. The expansion and prosperity of the kingdom is stated to be a fulfillment of the Word of the Lord spoken by Jonah the prophet. Thus it will be seen that Jonah was not only recognized as a prophet but the inference would be that it was possibly to a large extent through his ministry as a patriot and prophet that these things came to pass. This reference also makes it clear that Jonah was a historic character.

The name Jonah means 'dove' and the personal details known of him are that he was the son of Amittai of Gath-Hepher in Galilee near to Nazareth. This fact, incidentally, proves the wrong assumption of the Pharisees when they said "Out of Galilee arises no prophet" – see John 7: 52. In passing it may be mentioned that Nahum and Malachi were also of Galilee.

Prophets contemporary with Jonah were Joel to Judah and later Amos and Hosea to Israel. Jonah's ministry was confined to Israel; that is, the Northern Kingdom.

Both Jonah and the Book bearing his name have been subjected to much criticism designed to belittle its message and destroy its historicity. As has been stated above, Jonah is referred to as a historical person in 2 Kings 14: 25. Furthermore, the Lord Jesus Christ refers to Jonah in Matthew 12:39-41, where he teaches that Jonah was a type of his own coming, burial and resurrection. Moreover, the people of Nineveh are cited as examples of true repentance. Also observe the words of the Lord in Matthew 12: 41 "The men of Nineveh shall rise in judgment with this generation and shall condemn it…" Mythical characters will not rise in the judgment! This Book cannot be rejected simply because it contains the account of a miraculous happening, for one of the chief reasons why it has been preserved and given by the Holy Spirit is to illustrate and teach us something concerning the greater miracle of our Lord's resurrection.

The question will naturally arise as to why Jonah fled when first he had the message from God to go to Ninevah and cry against it – 1:1-3. Various reasons can be suggested in answer to this question, but first and foremost let it be said that it was not because Jonah was afraid to go to Nineveh. The story reveals him as a brave man, for in 1:12 he asked to be cast into the sea. In chapter 2 we read of him praying but not fainting in the midst of surroundings which must have been awesome and frightening to say the least. In chapter 3 he is to be seen preaching fearlessly in the center of the powerful enemy city.

No doubt he was influenced by his Jewish exclusivism and patriotism and he recognized Assyria as a powerful enemy; one to be feared as a cruel foe. The question may have arisen in his mind, why should God spare those people and why should they not be judged for their sin? Jonah no doubt saw the possibility of Nineveh's repentance and the nation being spared later to be the instrument in God's Hand to bring judgment upon His own nation of Israel.

Therefore, Jonah saw himself being used by God to preserve the nation destined to chastise Israel. Furthermore, he may have foreseen the possibility of repentance and, knowing God, he realized that the judgment he was commissioned to preach would not come to pass and therefore his own reputation as a prophet was at stake – see 4:2.

For whatever reason Jonah was at first disobedient, the Lord has overruled the incident that we might have this instructive Book which is full of typical and spiritual teaching.

MEMORIZE THE FOLLOWING DETAILS

KEY WORD – Go

KEY VERSE – 4:2

THEME – The Lord God is a God of grace to Gentile as well as to Jew.

NUMBER OF CHAPTERS – 4

The following is suggested as a brief Analysis of the Book:

The Prophet Commissioned and Disobedient	1
The Prophet Prays	2
The Prophet Recommissioned and Preaching	3
The Prophet Angry and Reproved	4

The Typical teaching of the Book is two-fold. Firstly, Jonah is a type of Christ and is directly applied by our Lord to Himself in Matthew 12:38-42.

Then secondly, the Book is typical of the history of Israel, for it illustrated their call and great privilege to be the heralds of God's message to the world. As the prophet Jonah was disobedient, so Israel as a nation have failed and been disobedient. They have been cast out and swallowed up by the nations, yet preserved within the nations, even as Jonah was swallowed by the great fish and yet preserved within the fish. Jonah was later vomited up and became a sign to the Gentile nation, as likewise in God's time and even in the generation in which we are living, Israel is being brought together again and in due time will be used by God to be the heralds of the message of His blessing to the world.

Please take particular note of Jonah's prayer in chapter 2 observing how many different Psalms he quotes. Does this teach or suggest that scripture should be quoted and used more often than it generally is in prayer?

Romans 3:29 is an apt commentary upon the outstanding message of the Book of Jonah. Turn to this scripture.

Arising from this Book the following truths are emphasized:

1. God's sovereignty at all times and over all circumstances; therefore, it is impossible to flee from Him.

2. God is not only the God of the Jews but of all men and therefore His love extends to all.

3. God is more righteous than man, for He knowing the king and people of Nineveh had the capacity to repent when given the opportunity therefore gave them that opportunity so that He might have mercy on such.

4. The longsuffering and infinite tenderness of the Lord is manifested, both in dealing with individuals such as Jonah and with a nation such as Assyria.

5. God's love and interest in one man, in this instance, in His servant Jonah. Therefore, he takes infinite pains and patience and overrules miraculously so that He might educate and fashion His servant and thus use him as an instrument in His hand.

QUESTIONS

1. Can you give the reference to Jonah in one of the Historical Books of the Old Testament and also what it says of the Prophet in that reference?

2. Give the meaning of the name 'Jonah.'

3. State from where Jonah came and comment on this with regard to the statement of the Pharisees in John 7:52.

4. State briefly how you would deal with the criticism that Jonah was not a historical character or that the events recorded in this Book are not strictly historical but only intended as an allegory.

5. Give the following details: Key Word, Key Verse, Theme and number of chapters.

6. Sum up the Book under three or four short headings.

7. Quote a Scripture from Paul's writing which sums up the outstanding message of The Book of Jonah.

MICAH

'Operation 39' – Lesson 33

In addition to the reading through the Book of Micah, read Isaiah chapters 7 & 8; Jeremiah 26:17-19. The historic background of the Prophet Micah and his times will be found in 2 Kings 15:8 – 20:21 and 2 Chronicles 27:1 – 32:33. This would have covered the period 756-695 B.C. It is recorded in Micah 1:1 that Micah prophesied during the reigns of Jotham, Ahaz and Hezekiah, kings of Judah. The contemporary kings of Israel were Pekahiah, Pekah and Hosea.

It will, therefore, be seen that Micah lived and prophesied in the Pre-exilic period of Hebrew history. He delivered his message to the Kingdoms of Judah and Israel.

The name Micah means "Who is like Jehovah" and the message of his Book reflects the meaning of his name even as this is summed up in the question of 7:18.

Contemporary with Micah was Isaiah in his ministry to Judah. Micah probably commenced his prophetic ministry some little time after the commencement of Isaiah's but when that Prophet was still ministering. There are several passages in the Books of Isaiah and Micah, which are similar and sometimes Micah has been referred to as a shortened edition of Isaiah. It is, however, a separate book and complete in itself. Hosea would have been the contemporary to Israel.

Micah came from the town of Moresheth-gath, a coastal town close to the Philistine border and situated at a strategic point on the route from Asia to Egypt. He would, therefore, see the many Embassies going down to Egypt, as for instance mentioned in Isaiah 30:1-7 and 31:1-3. He would be in a position to be conversant with the intrigues of the great powers of his day and so in a position to judge the state of affairs at Jerusalem. Although Micah came from Judah, his prophetic ministry was to both Judah and Israel and he was the only Prophet to direct his message to both kingdoms, hence you read in 1:1 the reference to Samaria and Jerusalem.

Although Micah and Isaiah were contemporary there are noticeable differences. For instance, Isaiah was a Prophet from the country but he declared unflinchingly the judgments of the Lord and reveals the corruption to be found in all classes of the nation in the princes, priests, prophets and people. Refer to such references as 1:2; 2:2,8,9 & 11; 3:1-3, 5, 11; 6:7-8.

MEMORIZE THE FOLLOWING DETAILS

KEY WORD – Hear

KEY PHRASE – The Lord's Controversy (to be found in 6:2)

KEY VERSES – 6:8; 7:18

NUMBER OF CHAPTERS – 7

It is possible to make a brief division of the Book as follows:

I. Denunciations – 1 – 3

II. Consolations – 4 – 7

The following is suggested as a fuller Analysis of the Book:

"The Lord's Controversy with His People"	
	Chapters
I. The People Called to Listen	1: 1 – 2: 13
• Warning of Coming Judgment	1: 2-16
• Reasons for Coming Judgment	2: 1-11
• Blessings Beyond the Coming Judgment	2: 12-13

II. The Rulers and Leaders Called to Listen	3: 1 – 5: 15
• The Sin of Princes, Prophets and Priests	3: 1-12
• Restoration and Blessing from the Lord	4: 1-8
• Israel's Travail	4: 9 – 5: 1
• Israel's Triumph	5: 2 – 5: 15
III. The Mountains Called to Listen	6: 1 – 7: 20
• The Lord Contends with His People	6: 1-12
• The Lord Delivers Sentence on His People	6: 13-16
• The Lord the Hope of His People	7: 1-20

Under each of the above three main headings there are to be found the following key phrases:

I. Hear all ye people – 1: 2

II. Hear O Heads of Jacob and ye Princes – 3: 1

III. Hear ye O mountains – 6: 2

Observe the use of the word 'hear' to draw special attention to the message that follows:

1:2; 3:1; 3:9; 6:1; 6:2

One of the outstanding passages found in the Book of Micah is the passage in chapter 5:2, where the birthplace of the coming Messiah is foretold. Thus it will be seen that Micah is the Prophet honored by God to make the announcement concerning the birthplace of the Lord Jesus. 5:2 is quoted in Matthew 2:5-6.

Micah has been called 'The Prophet of Hope' for although he is commissioned to preach judgment and does so with uncompromising faithfulness – see 3:12; 4:10; 6:16 – yet, nevertheless, promises are proclaimed as for instanced 2:12-13 and 4:1-8.

Reference has already been made above to passages in Micah which are similar to passages to be found in Isaiah and these can be traced with the aid of a concordance. Micah 4:6-7, is quoted by Zephaniah in

Zephaniah 3:19. In the New Testament refer to the following scriptures which are either quotations or allusions to the writing of Micah.

Matt. 2:5-6 – Micah 5:2

Matt. 10:35-36 – Micah 7:6

Mark 13:12 – Micah 7:6

Luke 12:53 – Micah 7:6

Compare Luke 1:73 with Micah 7:20.

Micah 3:12 is quoted in Jeremiah 26:18.

The Book of Micah is outstanding because of the many choice passages which it contains. All of the following should be carefully noted and you would do well to memorize several of them.

2: 13; 3:8; 4:3-4; 5:2; 6:7-8; 7:7-8; 7:18-19; 7:20

The closing verses; namely chapter 7:18-20, form the doxology of the Book. The Prophet has forewarned of judgment but sees beyond the coming doom and destruction and extols a God Who is without equal, One Who is a pardoning God, Who is a God of compassion and Who will perform that which He has promised.

QUESTIONS

1. What does the name 'Micah' mean? Is there any reference to the meaning of this name in this Book?

2. To which kingdom did the Prophet Micah minister? Give the approximate overall dates of his ministry.

3. Name other Prophets who were contemporary with Micah and his times.

4. Give the Key Word, Key Phrase and quote one or two Key verses from the Book of Micah.

5. Summarize the Book of Micah in two words, according to a rough division that can be made of his writings.

6. What is the outstanding prophecy in this Book?

7. Micah addresses himself to three groups in his message, making known the Lord's controversy with His people and calls upon these groups to listen. Name the groups.

8. There are several very choice verses in this Book. Name one that has spoken to you specially and briefly state its message to your own heart.

NAHUM

'Operation 39' – Lesson 34

Read the Book of Nahum more than once during the course of this study. It is difficult to state with any degree of certainty the times of Nahum but his historic background was, in all probability, within the period covered from 2 Kings 18:13 to 23:30, and 2 Chronicles 31:1 to 36:8.

The overall date of the period within which Nahum may have delivered his message would be from 690 – 606 B.C. and in all probability he prophesied towards the end of that period. Thebes, ancient capital of Upper Egypt on the Nile, referred to in the Book as 'No' – 3:8-10 – fell in 663 B.C. Nineveh fell in 606 B.C. and it seems almost certain that the prophecy directed against Ninevah was within this period and probably somewhere about central between the two dates. Nahum's prophecy was, therefore, Pre-exilic.

Contemporary with Nahum was the prophet Zephaniah. While there are those who believe that there was no prophetic ministry during the wicked reign of Manasseh, yet there are others who believe that both Nahum and Zephaniah broke the prophetic silence during that wicked reign.

In 1:1 Nahum is described as the Elkoshite and he was, therefore, a native of Elkosh. While there as an Elkosh in Syria a few miles north of the ruins of Nineveh and where it is claimed that the tomb of the prophet is to be found, yet others locate Elkosh as being in Galilee. This seems to be the more reasonable of these two suggestions. It has also been maintained that Elkosh was the previous name for Capernaum, for Nahum the prophet lived at Capernaum and hence the name – Kaphar Naum, that is, Nahum's Village. This last suggestion is an interesting one, but at any rate Nahum was a prophet to the Southern Kingdom of Judah.

In connection with the Book of the prophet Nahum read Isaiah 10 and also Zephaniah 2:13 – 3:7. No doubt in the course of these studies you have recently read the Book of Jonah. There is a close relationship between the two Books in view of the respective prophets' messages to Ninevah.

An appreciation of the historical position is helpful to a clear understanding of Nahum's prophecy which is concerned almost entirely with the pronouncement of the destruction and complete overthrow of Ninevah – although there is, at the same time, a message of comfort to the people of God. The Assyrian Empire had long held sway over the ancient world and was one that had been characterized by violence, cruelty and ruthlessness. No doubt at the time of the prophecy it appeared as if Ninevah would stand forever and its power be invincible. It is on record that the city of Ninevah had walls 100 feet high and were abroad enough for three chariots to drive abreast. The city had a circumference of 60 miles and was reinforced and guarded by more than 12000 towers. This is the mighty empire through which such names as Tiglath-Pileser, Shalmaneser, Sargon, Sennacherib, Esar-haddon and Asshur-banipal, had ruled the world, but following its destruction and God's judgment upon it, it is now impossible to state with certainty its site. An indication of the godless attitude of the Assyrians can be seen from the message delivered by their ambassador in the days of Hezekiah. Read the incident in 2 Kings 18:19 – 19:13 and then Isaiah's reply in 2 Kings 19:20-34.

It must also be remembered that to this city God had sent His prophet Jonah probably 15 years previously. At that time the King and the inhabitants had repented, but with the rising of new generations there had been a departure from this attitude. In its place there was open and deliberate blasphemy against the Lord as shown by the message delivered by Rab-Shakeh quoted in 2 Kings 18. Jonah's message was a call to repentance, now Nahum pronounced the irrevocable judgment and vengeance of the Lord against those who blasphemed His Name and dealt cruelly with His people.

The name Nahum means 'Comfort' or 'Consolation' and his prophecy is true to his name, for although he speaks of terrible judgment upon the enemies of the people of God, yet the fact that the Lord will deal thus with His adversaries is a comfort to the people of God. In the Book there are verses that speak of the Lord's delivering His people – 1:12-13 and 15. Also observe 1:3 and 7.

MEMORIZE THE FOLLOWING DETAILS

KEY WORD – Destruction

KEY PHRASE – An utter end

THEME – The Destruction of Nineveh.

KEY VERSES: 2:13; 3:5

NUMBER OF CHAPTERS – 3

Taking as a theme the judgment of God, the following analysis is suggested:

God's Judgment upon Ninevah Made Known	1
God's Judgment upon Nineveh Described	2
The Reason for God's Judgment upon Ninevah	3: 1-4
God's Judgment upon Nineveh Irrevocable and Complete	3: 5-19

Nahum writes in a style that is at once full of ardor and vivid, but nevertheless as he speaks of the judgments of the Lord there is a dignity and majesty which is in keeping with his subject. In particular, note the telling descriptions in chapter 2 of fire and flaming torches, of the overflowing river, of the sacking and ravaging of the city and of the lion destroying. Observe also in chapter 3 the vivid description of the battle – 3:2-3.

Make a special note of such passages as 1:3 and 1:7.

Observe the use of the phrase 'an utter end' – 1:8 and 1:9 – and 'Behold I am against thee, saith the Lord' – 2:13 and 3:5.

In 1:2-6, every word in the Hebrew Bible suggesting anger is used. This reveals something of the fierceness of the wrath of God against those who have known the truth but who have turned away from it and have deliberately blasphemed the Name of God and lifted up their hand against His people. This is God's reply to the proud and haughty Assyrian challenge recorded in 2 Kings 19:22-23.

As has been stated above, Nahum's name means 'Comfort' or 'consolation' for despite the fact that he delivers this Oracle against Ninevah he, nevertheless, 'a herald of hope' and his writing bring a message which is applicable today. World powers and forces that are based on force and evil may rise and claim to be invincible and overwhelming in their advance, yet God is still on the throne and He will remember His own.

You are asked to refer to Paul's quotation of 1:15 in Romans 10:15. The message of the Gospel brings the good tidings that Christ, by His death and resurrection, has once and for all made salvation and forgiveness available to His people. By His death on the cross that Lord has spoiled principalities and powers and defeated Satan, making a show of them openly and has broken their power forever – Colossians 2:14-15.

HABAKKUK

'Operation 39' – Lesson 35

The Book of Habakkuk should be read more than once during the course of this study, particular attention being focused upon chapter 3. The historic background to the Prophet and his writing will be found in 2 Kings 22:1 – 24:16 and 2 Chronicles 34:1 – 36:10. In all probability Habakkuk ministered during the latter part of the reign of Josiah and possibly in the reigns of Jehoahaz and Jehoiakim. It will, therefore, be seen that he is a Pre-exilic prophet.

The condition of the nation of Judah and the reference to the coming invasion by the Chaldeans indicates that the prophet wrote and spoke after the reformation which had been brought about by Josiah had begun to die out. Furthermore, it is clear that the power of the Assyrians had been broken and a new empire, the Babylonian Empire, was now rising rapidly and the invasion of Judah was imminent. The Overall dates of such a time would be 620 to 598 B.C. The prophet Jeremiah would be contemporary with Habakkuk.

Habakkuk was a prophet to the Southern Kingdom of Judah.

The name Habakkuk means 'Embracer', 'Wrestler', or 'To cling.' True to his name Habakkuk clung to God in prayer for the answer to the problems with which he was confronted.

From 3:1 and 3:19 it is suggested that he was a Levite engaged in leading the Temple singing. Habakkuk has been called 'an Interpreter of Providence' and 'the Prophet of faith.'

MEMORIZE THE FOLLOWING DETAILS

KEY WORDS: - Why, Woe, Wait

KEY VERSES – 1:13; 2:4; 2:20

NUMBER OF CHAPTERS – Three

It will be observed that approximately two thirds of the Book is taken up by conversation between the prophet and the Lord. The prophet states his problem; raises questions to which the Lord replies.

The prophet's first problem is concerned with the apostasy of Judah – 1:1-4. The Lord's reply is given in 1:5-11 in which He states that He is raising up and sending the Chaldeans on the people of Judah in judgment. This gives rise to the prophet's second problem, stated in 1:12 – 2:1. Habakkuk is perplexed as to how a pure God can use a cruel, ruthless foe as an instrument in His purposes. The Lord's reply is contained in 2:2-20. It is an answer which men must know; therefore, make it plain – 2:2. In the first instance, the just will be vindicated and the victory of the Lord will be complete, 2-14. Then further, God's sovereignty is supreme and He cannot and will not do that which does not accord with His love and holiness, 2:20.

The following is suggested as a brief Analysis of the Book:

Conversation 1	1:1-11
Conversation 2	1:12 – 2:20
The Prophet's Prayer, Praise and Doxology	3:1-19

A further Analysis of the Book can be stated as follows:

	Key Verse
The Sign of the Prophet in chapter 1	1:2
The Silence of the Prophet in chapter 2	2:20
The Song of the Prophet in chapter 3	3:18

There are several choice passages which deserve special thought and your attention is drawn in particular to the following verses; 1:13a; 2:1,2,3; 2:4; 2:18-19; 2:20; 3:2; 3:17-18; 3:19

The description of the might, majesty and revelation of the Lord God in chapter 3 is one of the great passages of the Old Testament – therefore read it and reread it.

Among the passages to which your attention has been drawn in the paragraph above, you will observe the phrase in 2:4 – 'The just shall live by his faith.' This must have been one of the Apostle Paul's favorite quotations, for we find him using it in Romans 1:17 and Galatians 3:11. It is also quoted again in Hebrews 10:38. Turn to these three New Testament passages and observe that in Romans 1:17 the word emphasized is 'just'; in Galatians 3:11 the emphasis is on 'faith'; and in Hebrews 10:38 the emphasis is on 'live.'

Paul quotes Habakkuk 1:5 in delivering his warning to unbelieving Jews in Antioch as recorded in Acts 13:41.

Martin Luther acted upon the quotation 'the just shall live by faith' in Gal. 3:11. It will be seen therefore that the message of the Book Habakkuk had an important part in bringing about the Reformation.

Your attention is also directed to the five 'Woes' pronounced against the Chaldeans in chapter 2.

In this Book the Prophet's faith is revealed as being Tested, Taught and finally Triumphant. Read and reread 3:17-18. The nation was going from bad to worse and the invading armies would soon march through the land and judgment from the Lord would come, yet it was still true that the lord was in His holy temple and therefore the just shall be kept and shall live by his faith, and in view of this the prophet says 'Yet I will rejoice in the Lord, I will joy in the God of my salvation.'

QUESTIONS

1. Give the meaning of the name Habakkuk.

2. Give the Key Words, Key Verses and number of chapters in the Book of Habakkuk.

3. Was Habakkuk a pre-exilic or post-exilic Prophet?

4. Give one of the special characteristics of this Book.

5. Quote one of the best known phrases found in this Book, which is recorded three times in the New Testament. Give the New Testament references.

6. Choose one of the several choice scriptures to which your attention has been drawn in the lesson notes. State why you have chosen same, and what its message has been to your own heart.

ZEPHANIAH

'Operation 39' – Lesson 36

You will be able to read through the short Book of the Prophet Zephaniah more than once during the course of this study. The historic background will be found in references to 2 Kings 22:1 – 24:7 and 2 Chronicles 34:1 – 37:8. In Zephaniah 1:1 the prophet states that he prophesied in the days of Josiah King of Judah. The date would, therefore, be approximately 640 – 610 B.C.

Zephaniah gives also in 1:1 his genealogy and Hizkiah is usually taken as referring to the King Hezekiah, so that the prophet would appear by descent to be a prince of the royal house of Judah. The name of Zephaniah means 'he who Jehovah hides' or 'hidden of Jehovah.' See 2:3 where the prophet uses a play on his name to enforce his message.

It has been stated above, Zephaniah prophesied in the reign of King Josiah. There can be little doubt that it was primarily due to Zephaniah's ministry that the Revival took place during king Josiah's reign. Contemporary prophets would have been, Nahum just immediately prior to Zephaniah, and later Jeremiah. Zephaniah was a prophet to the Southern Kingdom of Judah prior to the Captivity in Babylon, that is, Pre-exilic.

Although Zephaniah's prophecy lacks something of the majesty and rhythm to be found in certain other prophetic books, nevertheless it pronounces judgment and foretells restoration in no uncertain way, and in particular the following two passages should be compared and contrasted:

1:14-18 The Certainty of Judgment 3:14-17 The Joy and Blessedness of Salvation

MEMORIZE THE FOLLOWING DETAILS

KEY WORDS – Visitation and Restoration - 1:14 and 3:20

KEY VERSES – 1:14 and 3:30

NUMBER OF CHAPTERS – Three

One of the most frequent phrases used in the Book is the phrase 'the day of the Lord' – It is used seven times referring to Judgment. No more vivid description of the Day of the Lord (which is referred to by most of the prophets) is to be found than that in this Book, namely – 1:14-18.

Observe also the phrase 'the Lord is in the midst' – 3:5; 3:12; 3:15; 3:17. Also observe such references as 2:14 and 3:12.

Also note the use of the word 'jealousy' – 1:18 and 3:8. The jealousy of the Lord is declared! God so loves His own people that He seeks their wholehearted devotion and cannot be satisfied with anything less than this. Therefore, this Book has a pertinent message to the people of God today. God loves with an everlasting love and seeks that His own love Him in full and glad surrender, which implies also a ready obedience and willingness to do His will.

A simple, two-fold Analysis of the Book is as follows:

	Chapters
I. The Lord is in the Midst for Judgment	1:1 – 3:8
• Judgment upon Judah	1:1-18
• Judgment upon Gentile Nations	2:4 – 3:8
II. The Lord is in the Midst for Salvation	3:9-20

The following Analysis will also be found to be helpful:

	Chapters
I. The Day of Wrath is at Hand	1:1 – 3:8a
• Retribution – from the Lord	1: 1-18
• Repentance – 'seek ye the Lord'	2:1-3
• Desolation of the Nations by the Lord	2:4-15
• The Sin of Jerusalem – in the sight of the Lord	3:1-8a
II. The Day of Blessing Foretold	3:9-20
• Salvation of the Nations	3:9-10
• Restoration of Israel	3:11-13
• Jubilation of the Redeemed	3:14-17
• Re-establishment and Consummation of Original Purpose	3:18-20

Thus it will be seen that the Book commences with the pronouncement of Judgment and Woe but ends with a Song of Joy and Triumph – 3:14-17. Indeed, the last section of the Book has been called 'the sweetest love song in the Old Testament.'

QUESTIONS

1. During which king's reign did Zephaniah prophesy and what was an outstanding event in this reign which is usually attributed to Zephaniah's ministry?

2. To which kingdom did Zephaniah prophesy?

3. Give the meaning of the name 'Zephaniah.'

4. Quote one of the phrases which is used frequently in the Book.

5. What name has been applied to the last section of the Book?

6. State two contrasting messages which are found in this Book.

7. Give the Key words, Key verses and number of chapters.

HAGGAI

'Operation 39' – Lesson 37

After you have read the Book of the Prophet Haggai right through, read again the Book message by message according to the Analysis given later in these notes.

The Three Prophets Haggai, Zechariah and Malachi prophesied after the return of the people of God to the Promised Land following their captivity in Babylon. These Prophets are, therefore, known as Post-exilic Prophets.

It will be recalled that when the people of God first returned from Babylon they set to and laid the foundation of the Temple but as a result of opposition from the Samaritans and other enemies the work was hindered and then discontinued for fourteen or fifteen years. The historic background is contained in the Book of Ezra chapters 1 to 6. In particular note Ezra 5:1-2 and 6:14-15. In these passages Haggai and Ezra are associated as being primarily responsible for the recommencement of the work of building the Temple.

In 1:1 Haggai states that the Word of the Lord came to him in the second year of Darius and this would have been 520 B.C. Each message in the Book is dated and from these it will be seen that the prophecies contained in the writing of Haggai were delivered within a period of three months and twenty-four days; namely, September to December, 520 B.C.

The name Haggai means 'my feast' or 'festal.' He has been called 'a Minister of Encouragement.' In all probability he came from the priestly family, for 2:10-14 suggest close connection with the priests, and was undoubtedly among the exiles that returned from Babylon where he would have been born during the time of the Captivity.

Although the returned exiles had at first been stopped through the hostility and enmity of the Samaritans, with the lapse of time the desire to rebuild the Temple had grown less. When Haggai and Zechariah delivered their messages, the people had begun to settle themselves into the land and were busy in building their own fine houses and thus could not find time for the work of the House of the Lord. There had been natural calamities, such as draught and mildew, and the two prophets are sent by God to deliver a message of rebuke and encouragement, and to interpret these natural happenings to the people. Their ministry was so effective that within twenty-four days the people began to rebuild the Temple and it is with a note of triumph that Ezra records in Ezra 6:14 – "They built and finished it according to the command of the God of Israel … and this house was finished…..!"

Haggai's style is very business-like and to the point. To enforce his message, he frequently asks questions. In your study of the Book observe every question he asks, as, for instance, in 1:4; 1:9; 2:3 (in which there are three questions), 2:12; 2:13; 2:19.

MEMORIZE THE FOLLOWING DETAILS

KEY WORDS – Consider

KEY PHRASES – "Consider your way" "Build the house" "The Word of the Lord"

KEY VERSES – 1:5, 7

NUMBER OF CHAPTERS – Two

Study the following Analysis which is based on the five messages declared by the Prophet. Observe that each of these is dated, as follows:

| First message | September 1st |
| Second message | September 24th |

Third message	October 21st
Fourth message	December 24th
Fifth message	December 24th

First Message	A Call to Action – the People Reproved	1:1-11
Second Message	A Promise of the Lord's Presence and Commendation – the People Commenced the Work	1:12-15
Third Message	A Call to Courage – Supporting the People in the Work	2:1-9
Fourth Message	A Call to Cleansing and Patience – Declaring the Blessing	2:10-19
Fifth Message	A Call to Hope – Declaring the Promise	2:20-23

Mark in your Bible or notes in some particular way the many times there is reference to the phrases "the Word of the Lord" and "saith the Lord of Hosts," "the voice of the Lord" and similar phrases. Was this the secret of the effectiveness of the message of the Prophet? He came as a man with the authority and message of the Lord.

Also observe the use of the word "consider" – 1:5; 1:7; 2:15; 2:18.

Note too, the use of short, dynamic phrases such as "be strong," "fear ye not."

The Prophet Haggai was sent by God to deal with the slothfulness and despondency which had settled upon the people of God. He called upon the people of his day to judge aright, for though there was increasing prosperity and much labor was being bestowed upon seeking comfort and security, yet the outcome was increasing insecurity and lack of satisfaction; for instance see 1:6. Hence the main message of the Prophet is to call upon the people to build the house. Everything else must take second place to the work of the Lord. Self-advancement, self-interest, self-security, must take a back place and in seeking to do the will of the Lord there is the promise of true prosperity and security as, for instance, 2:18-19 and 23.

Haggai was not only a great preacher and prophet but also a real worker – see Ezra 5:1-2. From the reference to him in the Book of Ezra and from what may be gathered from his Book, there is much that the Christian worker can learn with profit. He was a man with a message and a mission! Haggai 2: 6 is quote in Hebrews 12:26-27. This would appear to be the only quotation in the New Testament from Haggai. The Temple that was built at this time, although restored and almost rebuilt by Herod the Great, was the Temple to which the Lord came in the days of His flesh.

Tradition associates the following Psalms as coming from the pen of Haggai:

Psalms 111, 125, 126, 127, 146, 147, 148; but it cannot be stated definitely whether or not the Prophet wrote all of these Psalms, yet as you read them they are vibrant with just such a message as you would expect from this Prophet.

ZECHARIAH

'Operation 39' – Lesson 38

Your reading of the Book of Zechariah will need time, thought and care, and if possible you should read it through more than once during the course of this study. In addition, read or refer to Ezra chapters 1-6. Zechariah is also mentioned in Nehemiah 12:4 and 16.

The date of Zechariah's first prophecy would be 520 B.C. In all probability the latter part of the Book contains his prophecy or message of later years. He was contemporary with Haggai but evidently a younger man - See 2:4. He would almost certainly have been born in captivity in Babylon and returned under Zerubbabel. Both Zechariah and Haggai prophesied in the second year of Darius. Zechariah is, therefore, a Post-exilic Prophet.

Personal details of the Prophet are given in 1: 1 where it is stated that Zechariah was the son of Berechiah, the son of Iddo the Prophet. Compare this with Ezra 5:1; 6:14; and Nehemiah 12: 4,6. The fact that there other passages do not refer to Berechiah probably means that Berechiah his father died when Zechariah was still young and hence the emphasis on his grandfather Iddo, who was also a Prophet.

The three names given in 1: are significant. Zechariah means 'The Lord remembers;' Berecchiah 'the Lord blesses' and Iddo means 'appointed time' or 'timely.' Thus it will be seen that a combination of these three names forms the theme of the Book. The Lord remembers, the Lord blesses and always at the right time. Zechariah was a Priest as well as a Prophet.

Zechariah commenced his ministry two months after that of Haggai. Compare 1:1 with Ezra 5:1; 6:14 and Haggai 1:1. The early part of his ministry lasted two years and if he wrote the latter part of the Book, as is generally thought when he was a much older man it is conceivable that he would have been alive in Nehemiah's day. The following is a comparison of the prophecies of Haggai and the early prophecies of Zechariah:

520 B.C	September	Haggai	1:1-11
	October	Haggai	2:1-9
	November	Zechariah	1:1-6
	December	Haggai	2:10-19
519 B.C.	January	Zechariah	1:7 – 6:15
518 B.C.	November	Zechariah	7:1 – 8:23

The temple was completed in 516 and the ministry of the two Prophets was designed to encourage the people of God to continue with the rebuilding of the temple. Their ministry was most effective and the one Prophet forms a fitting compliment to the other. Haggai was practical, forthright, even to the point of bluntness, whereas Zechariah is more poetical and as will be seen within the Book was granted visions by the Lord which are to be passed on to the people. Thus by these two Prophets who were so totally different, God brings encouragement to a despondent people. Particularly in the case of Zechariah, the message is to look away from the present and immediate to the future and the possibilities that God has in store for those who trust and obey Him.

Zechariah can, therefore, be called 'the Prophet of Encouragement.'

It will, however, be seen that while Zechariah has a message for his own day and generation, it also has further application to Israel in the future and also to the church in the present. He surveys the whole of Messianic Prophecy dealing with the coming and character of the Lord Jesus, also speaking of His rejection, sufferings, His second coming, acceptance and glorious reign. Thus both advents of our Lord are referred to in this Book. This is the probably reason why Zechariah is quoted frequently in the New Testament.

You will also observe that the Prophet is instructed by means of visions from the Lord and in these visions and elsewhere in the Book there is considerable use of symbols. In some instances the symbols are interpreted within the Book itself and it is always helpful to turn to the use of the same symbols in other parts of scripture in seeking to understand their meaning. By reason of these visions and symbols The Book of Zechariah has been called the 'Apocalypse of the Old Testament.'

One simple division of the Book would be into two sections as follows:

1. Apocalyptic – chapters 1 – 8
2. Prophetic – chapters 9 – 14

In seeking to understand and also derive the greatest possible help from this Book two points need to be emphasized. Firstly, that its message is one that can be applied today. Secondly, certain sections have their immediate fulfillment yet probably the greater part has yet to find final fulfillment and particularly in its application to Israel and the coming again of Christ the Messiah.

It has been suggested in certain quarters that chapters 1-8 and chapters 9-14 are by different authors. This is principally on account of the change of style. It is, however, no proof of change of authorship for the subject matter is completely different. The first part of the Book contains the visions intended to reassure and encourage the people of God to continue with the immediate task of rebuilding the Temple and establishing themselves in the land. The latter part of the Book speaks of judgment because of the coming rejection of their Messiah followed by His return and the establishment of the Messianic kingdom. The Jewish tradition is also to the effect that the first part of Zechariah was written when he was a young man and latter part 30 or 40 years after the visions so one would expect a difference in style between a burning young Prophet and the same Prophet as an old man. The objection raised against the latter part of the Book as being the work of Zechariah because it refers to the power and conflict with Greece in 9:13 is not valid. It is true that Greece was not at that time a world power but that fact does not preclude the Prophet pronouncing conflict and judgment on Greece at a future time.

Zechariah 11:12-13 is quoted in Matthew 27:9-10 and there the quotation is attributed to Jeremiah. There was a saying among the Jews that 'the spirit of Jeremiah rests upon Zechariah' so that it is quite conceivable that Zechariah took one of the familiar sayings or prophecies of Jeremiah and quoted it, as indeed it is stated in Zechariah 7:7 'why should they not turn to the Prophets of old?'

MEMORIZE THE FOLLOWING DETAILS

KEY WORDS – Restoration and Glory

KEY VERSE – 4:6

NUMBER OF CHAPTERS – 14

The Book may be Analyzed briefly according to the five principal messages of the Book set out as under:

First message	1:1-6
Second message	1:7 – 6:15
Third message	7:1 – 8:23
Fourth message	9:1 – 11:17
Fifth message	12:1 – 14:21

The following summary may also be helpful:

The Call to Repentance and to Turn unto the Lord	1:1-6
Visions of Restoration to Correct Wrong Outlook	1:7 – 6:8
A Symbolic Act	6:9-15
Oracles of Appeal	7:1 – 8:23
The Disclosing of Destiny	9:1 – 14:21

Your attention is specially directed to the eight visions that were granted in one night to the Prophet Zechariah. There are as follows:

The angelic horseman	1:7-17
The four horns and four blacksmiths	1:18-21
The man with the measuring line	2
Joshua the high priest	3
The golden candlestick and olive trees	4
The flying roll	5:1-4
The Ephah and the woman	5:5-11
The four chariots and horsemen	6:1-8

The meaning of these visions as applicable both to Israel and to the Church and believers is probably on the following lines.

- God is in the shadows but is not unmindful of His own and will fulfill His promises.

- Every adversary and difficulty will be adequately dealt with and overthrown by God.

- Beware of trying to limit or measure God's work. His purposes far exceed every expectation.

- This speaks of the removal of iniquity and the sufficiency of God's remedy to deal with the past.

- The people of God are called upon to be His witnesses and He has made an exhaustless supply of oil in the person of the Holy Spirit for this purpose.

- No doubt a reference to the Word of God and the provisions of His Word for holy living.

- The Ephah was a commercial measure of three measures of meal and its removal signifies the removal of wickedness and injustice from the people of God.

- Speaks of God's sovereignty and government and is intended to reassure the heart that God is still on the throne. No doubt this has particular application to God's dealings with those nations and people who have persecuted and caused such suffering to the Jews.

The symbolic act recorded in chapter 6:9-15 foreshadows the coming and the crowning of the Priest-King, of whom Joshua the high Priest is but a shadow. Particularly observe the words in 6:12 "behold the man" and compare with the words of Pilate in John 19:5. It is noteworthy that Joshua is the Hebrew equivalent for Jesus.

In chapters 7 and 8 the Prophet deals with various questions which have been asked concerning certain fasts which had been instituted on the downfall of Jerusalem. Now that the Temple is rebuilt the question arises as to whether these fasts should still be kept. Observe the answers given in 7:1-7; 7:8-14; 8:1-7; 8:18-23. The people are invited to examine the motive of their fasting and also whether it has been accompanied by true justice and compassion and goes on to speak of the restoration and prosperity that awaits the people of God, so that fasting will be turned to feasting – 8:19.

Your attention is specially directed to the following scriptures referring to Christ:

The Lord is referred to as the 'Branch'	3:8; 6:12
The coming of the King to Jerusalem (Quoted Matt. 21:5)	9:9
The price paid and the casting of it away	11:12-13
The wounding and slaying of the Shepherd	13:6-7
The scattering of His people	13:7
The Second Coming of Christ and the repentance and cleansing of Israel	12:9-13:1
The Second Coming of Christ	14:3-8

In the later part of the Book there are also repeated references to the conquest and victory of the Lord and the Book concludes on the glad glorious note of the cleansing complete and the Messiah triumphant – 14:20-21.

QUESTIONS

1. Give the approximate date of Zechariah's firm prophecy, and explain why the latter part of his Book varies in style from the earlier part.

2. Give the meaning of the name 'Zechariah.'

3. Give the name of any Prophet or Prophets contemporary with Zechariah.

4. Briefly sum up the Book in two divisions.

5. State the purpose of the visions recorded in the opening six chapters.

6. Describe the eight visions in eight short phrases.

7. The Book of Zechariah contains many prophecies concerning Christ. State which these are.

MALACHI

'Operation 39' – Lesson 39

We now come to the last Book of the Old Testament and you are asked to read it through in conjunction with Nehemiah chapters 8 to 13, taking particular note of Nehemiah chapters 12 and 13.

The probable date of this prophecy is within the period 435 – 400 B.C. and the state of affairs described in the Book of Malachi are the same as the conditions which prevailed at Jerusalem when Nehemiah returned to the city and discovered that the earlier revival had died down. In its place there was a growing departure from God, irregularities in the Temple worship and the priests were behaving themselves in an unbecoming manner. The people were neglectful of tithes and offerings. Marriages with heathen wives had become a common; Jewish wives being divorced so as to permit this. The reformation and revival under Nehemiah when he first came to Jerusalem had been more or less completely forgotten. It is to these conditions that the message of Malachi is directed.

The name Malachi means 'my messenger.' No personal details are known of this Prophet. He was certainly true to his name and was sent by the Lord as the Lord's messenger. There are those who believe that the name Malachi was either an assumed name or a name applied to him by reason of his utterance. He is not referred to elsewhere in the Old Testament or in the New Testament by name. What Haggai and Zechariah were to Zerubbabel of an earlier generation, so too was Malachi the messenger of Jehovah to Nehemiah. He was, therefore, a Post-exilic Prophet.

In addition to the use of the name 'my messenger' or 'the messenger' in 1:1, three times within the Book this name is introduced; first of all it is applied to the messenger of the Lord of hosts – 2:7; then in chapter 3 there is reference to 'my messenger.' In 3:1 it is used referring to John the Baptist; and again in the same verse, 3:1, 'the messenger of the Covenant' – a reference to the Lord Jesus. There is also a further reference to the coming of Elijah the Prophet – 4:5. This last refers either to John the Baptist or a Prophet of the Lord who has yet to be revealed.

Malachi has been referred to as 'the unknown prophet,' 'a Preacher of Destiny.' It is fitting that the Old Testament should close with the writing of this messenger of the Lord. It is a prophecy that demands special consideration as containing a message to the people of God today.

MEMORIZE THE FOLLOWING DETAILS

KEY WORD – Apostasy

KEY PHRASES – 'Yet ye say' 'I have loved you, saith the Lord'

KEY VERSE – 1:2

NUMBER OF CHAPTERS – Four

The following is a brief Analysis of the Book:

I. A Declaration of Love	1: 1-5
II. A Message of Rebuke	1:6 – 2:16
• To the Priests	1:6 – 2:9
• To the People	2:10-16
III. A Declaration of Destiny	2:17 – 4:6
• The Certainty of the Advent	2:17 – 3:1
• Cleansing for the Lord's People	3:2,4
• Judgment for the Unrighteous	3:3-6
• The Promises for, and Preserving of, the Lord's People	3:7-18
• The Two Destinies Revealed	4:1-6
Burning for the Wicked	
Healing for the Righteous	

As you read the Book through you will observe the form of dialogue between the Lord and the people. The people constantly raise questions and question the Lord's actions, revealing their critical spirit. This is always evident in the case of those who are apostatizing or backsliding in their relationship with the Lord, hence the phrase 'yet ye say,' to be found in 1:2,3,4,12,13; 2:14,17; 3:7,8,13,14. Also observe the use of the word 'wherein,' 1:2,6,7; 2:17; and 3:7,8,13. The people are not prepared to admit their unfaithfulness as they are rebuked by the Lord through the Prophet. Their hardness of heart is revealed by their readiness and desire to argue with the Lord. This is characteristic of the church which has become spiritually dead and of the backsliding believer. Today there is an unwillingness to recognize where the Church has departed from first love and true devotion to the Lord. Hence the message of Malachi is a message for today.

The message of this Book is largely to those who are religious without being righteous.

Your attention is again directed to the fact that Malachi is referred to as 'a Preacher of Destiny.' The two destinies are clearly set forth in chapters 3 and 4. For the Lord's own it is to be spared and counted as the Lord's special treasure and healed; for those who resist God and do wickedly, there is destruction referred to as 'burning as in an oven or furnace.'

There are many choice passages to be found within this Book. Observe and mark such verses as 1:11; 2:5-6; 3:1-3; 3:6; 3:8; 3:10-11; 3:16-18; 4:2. Be on the lookout for the vivid expressions which are also used, such as when the Prophet reminds the people of their waywardness, for instance in 3:13 – "your words have been stout against me, saith the Lord,"

The Book opens with a declaration of the love of God for His people and closes with the pronouncement of the smiting with a curse. The message of Malachi can, therefore, be summed up: 'remember the love of God, repent of your sins, return to the Lord and speak often of His love and His grace and His promise to come to receive His own.' The promise is sure! Just as surely as Christ came, in fulfillment of the promise, to Bethlehem, so the Church today has the promise of His coming again. The promise is sure and the Lord will come suddenly to His Temple.

It is significant to observe that the first Book of the Old Testament closes with a reference to a coffin and the last Book of the Old Testament closes with reference to the curse – both the curse and the coffin coming as a direct result of the sin of man. Throughout the Old Testament there is the story of man's sin and failure, but with the promise of the coming of the Second Man, the Last Adam, the Lord from Heaven, Who came to give life and life more abundantly, so that there might be no more death and no more curse. Thus redeemed and forgiven sinners are enabled to enter into fellowship with God and be sharers of His righteousness and glory.

QUESTIONS:

1. Give the probable date of the period during which the Prophet Malachi prophesied.

2. Which Historical Book of the Old Testament deals with the same period in Hebrew history?

3. Give the meaning of the name 'Malachi.'

4. State in what way the Prophet introduces the meaning of his own name into the Book?

5. Write out the Key Word, Key Phrases and Key Verse of the Book of Malachi.

6. Give three headings which sum up the contents of the Book.

7. Give one of the favorite phrases which is used in the Book and which reveals the attitude of the people.

8. How would you state the message of Malachi as applicable today?

9. Malachi has been referred to by one or two other titles. Give two of these and explain why they are applied to the Prophet.

ACKNOWLEDGMENTS

The following people made it possible for this book to be printed: Chris O'Byrne, Rae Kuddle, Debbie O'Byrne, American friends in the area, and last but not least, my husband, Michael. There is no more important book in the world to study than the Holy Bible. In light of the current worldwide pandemic (COVID-19), my prayer is that people will have time and the desire to use this helpful study guide and delve into God's Word. May this start a habit of study that will remain long after the pandemic passes.

ABOUT THE TRANSCRIBER MIRIAM MARANZENBOIM

Originally from Temple City, California, Miriam Maranzenboim came from a spiritually well-fed church called Hope Union Church in Rosemead, California. Deeply impacted by four different speakers from the "Torchbearers," Miriam told her parents that she wanted to study at Capernwray Bible School in England. Quite taken aback ('Aren't our Bible schools here in the USA good enough?'), they agreed to let their 19-year-old daughter attend. Miriam earned her way and actually found another person from Southern California with whom to travel. The impact of what she learned is reflected by a passing comment, "If there had been a fire, I would have grabbed my notes from Capernwray!" Miriam attended the 1965 fall session and the "first-time-offered" 1966 spring session. At the end of the course she purchased additional supplementary notes and has kept them well over 54 years! She views these notes as a rare and wonderful aid to studying the Word of God.

The author of four other books, including the well-received "Josephus: The History of the Jews Condensed in Simple English," Miriam lives in Haifa, Israel with her refusenik husband of 40 years.

www.ingramcontent.com/pod-product-compliance
Lightning Source LLC
Chambersburg PA
CBHW070140100426
42743CB00013B/2777